FINANCES AFTER 55:
Make the Transition from Earning a Living to Retirement Living

FINANCES AFTER 55:
Make the Transition from Earning a Living to Retirement Living

Sylvia Lim, CFP®, CGA

Self-Counsel Press
(a division of)
International Self-Counsel Press Ltd.
USA   Canada

Self-Counsel Press acknowledges the financial support of the Government of Canada through the Book Publishing Industry Development Program (BPIDP) for our publishing activities.

Printed in Canada

First edition: 2005

Library and Archives Canada Cataloguing in Publication

Lim, Sylvia
    Finances after 55: make the transition from earning a living to retirement living/Sylvia Lim. — 1st ed.

    (Self-counsel reference series)
    ISBN 1-55180-582-0

    1. Retirement income—Planning. I. Title. II. Title: Finances after fifty-five. III. Series.

HG179.L548 2005   332.024'014   C2004-907289-7

Self-Counsel Press
(a division of)
International Self-Counsel Press Ltd.

1704 N. State Street	1481 Charlotte Road
Bellingham, WA 98225	North Vancouver, BC V7J 1H1
USA	Canada

CONTENTS

NOTICE TO READERS

The author, the publisher, and the vendor of this book make no representation or warranties regarding the outcome or the use to which the information in this book is put and are not assuming any liability for any claims, losses, or damages arising out of the use of this book. The reader should not rely on the author or the publisher of this book for any professional advice. Please be sure that you have the most recent edition.

Worksheets, Checklists and a Glossary are included on Self-Counsel Press's website at <www.self-counsel.com/updates/after55/bonus.htm>. Worksheets 1 and 9, and Checklists 1 through 3 are in MS Word and PDF formats. Worksheets 2 through 8 are in Microsoft Excel and PDF formats. The MS Word and Microsoft Excel files are workable files, which means you can work on and save the forms on your Windows PC. If you don't have these programs on your computer, you can print the PDF files and fill them in by hand.

Chapter 1
WHY PLAN?

Whether you're retiring solo or as part of a couple, planning is the key to a successful retirement, and it's never too late to start your planning. You may be 16 years away from retirement, or only 6 years, or maybe even already 6 months into your post-working life, and yet it's still possible for you to benefit from a plan.

The best candidate for the job of creating your plan is you, as you have your own best interests at heart. And, after all, you have the rest of your life to look after, and no one will take better care of your retirement finances than you will — provided you know what you're doing.

This chapter examines the reasons for creating a retirement plan, including our increasing longevity and our need for financial independence. It also examines our common fears of retirement and old age that can keep us from planning and discusses how to successfully overcome them, and concludes with an examination of the three phases of retirement: active, semi-active, and passive — and how each may be approached successfully.

Statistics

Those facing retirement today and for the next two decades are the baby boomers: people who were born between 1947 and 1966. They represent the biggest slice of the total North American population today, and they are also one of the wealthiest groups in the population base. (However, the baby boom was not an international phenomenon. The only other countries that experienced any kind of a post-war baby boom aside from the United States and Canada were Australia and New Zealand.)

Baby boomers are living longer and healthier lives than the people of past generations. In fact, the life expectancy of retirees has more than doubled in the last 25 years. No doubt life expectancy will continue to grow as more breakthroughs occur in biotechnology and health sciences. New discoveries every day are enabling the baby boomers and their parents not only to lead longer lives, but also to enjoy vastly improved quality of daily living.

American demographics

In 2003, there were almost 35 million people aged 65 years and older (Source: AoA). This number represented 12.3 percent of the total population, or about one in eight Americans.

There were another 25.3 million younger baby boomers between the ages of 55 and 64, or 8.9 percent of the population (about one in eleven Americans).

It is projected that by the year 2030, the number of people of the aging baby-boom generation more than 65 years of age will total an astonishing 71.5 million, representing 20 percent of the US population, or about one in five Americans.

The projected rapid growth of the over-65 population will continue to raise concerns about the overall social and economic condition of the American population. Already, there are grumblings from government sources saying that current levels of spending in social security and health care cannot be sustained. However, there is hope that the changing demographics will also give rise to technological breakthroughs and new assistive developments that can help ease the burdens of daily living for the seniors in our population. Assistive technologies have come a long way in helping people live more independent lives, thereby easing the burden of governments to care for a growing aging population in institutions. Assistive technology includes devices and services that help people in their activities in daily living (ADL), so that they can stay independent and integrate comfortably into their homes and communities. Some popular examples include electrically adjustable beds, walk-in bathtubs (with grab bars), and voice-command electronic devices. All are designed with the aging boomer and their parents in mind.

According to the US Federal Reserve Board's most recent Survey of Consumer Finances, the average net worth for households headed by people aged 55 to 64 is $530,000, while that for those in the 65 to 74 age group is $465,000. These are the highest of all the age groups as tracked by the Federal Reserve Board.

They also owe the least amount of debt in American households. The average debt is $74,000 for households headed by people aged 55 to 64, while debt for those in the 65 to 74 age group is even less, at $53,000.

Canadian demographics

As in the United States, Canada also has a large baby-boom population. Baby boomers make up by far the largest percentage of the Canadian population. The average Canadian baby boomer at present is somewhere in his or her 50s. This group is one of the wealthiest in the Canadian population base, and it is also the best educated. If not contemplating early retirement, many Canadian baby boomers are already enjoying it in great numbers.

Retirees make up one of the fastest growing groups in Canada. According to Statistics Canada, by the year 2010, more than 14 percent of the population will be aged 65 years or more. By 2020, that group will increase to more than 18 percent of the total population, and its growth shows no sign of slowing. By 2030, almost one in four Canadians (or 25 percent) will be 65 or older.

Life expectancy is steadily on the rise. Canadians are gaining two to three years of life with every passing decade. For an average Canadian male currently aged 55 years, life expectancy is 80 years. For an average Canadian female of the same age, life expectancy is 84 years. (Source: Report on the demographic situation in Canada 2002.)

Canadian seniors also appear to be much more financially secure than their predecessors, if wealth (and not just income) is included in the equation. Surprisingly, more than 73 percent of senior households have no debt. In the past 15 years, income for seniors has risen faster than income for those less than age 65. In fact, half of all seniors are living within their means, suggesting that savings continue well into their retirement years. (Source: Statistics Canada.)

Caregiver demographics

According to the Conference Board, there are now seven million Americans who are caring for their aging parents. In a few years, almost 40 percent of all US workers will be more involved with caring for a parent than for a child. In Canada, four-and-a-half million family caregivers provide greater than 80 percent of all home care.

The majority of these caregivers are women. Most of them are spouses and daughters. Often, these women are also caring for their own children — hence the term "sandwich generation," meaning someone who is sandwiched between the two generations, caring for dependent children and dependent parents. However, not all caregivers are women. Surprisingly, husbands make up nearly half of all caregivers over age 75.

By 2010, 60 percent of adults over age 50 will have a surviving parent, compared to only 16 percent in 1960.

In both the US and Canada, the implications of all of these statistics are enormous. New industries will rise up or evolve to service this growing market, and governments will have to become more innovative in delivering services to this sector of the population. The individual, however, must emphasize early planning for his or her retirement needs, and look at ways to support his or her longer life span and changing lifestyle.

The Fear Factor

Many people fear retirement.

To some, it means aging, and in today's youth-oriented culture, age is not seen as desirable. Others may view retirement as a loss of independence or power. And for those who have already retired, it may symbolize a loss of status and financial security.

As we get older, we may fear that our grown children will be burdened by our increased physical dependence. Along with this fear comes the fear of loss of respect from loved ones.

Fear of developing chronic illnesses is another factor. Again, it will mean becoming more dependent on others and having less control over our own lives and destinies. Fear of falling also comes into play here. It's been proven that many serious injuries are the result of accidental falls. Many elders become incapacitated and never fully recover their former mobility and independence.

Another big fear for many people is running out of money to support themselves. The image of an old person begging for money, living on the street, and eating in soup kitchens can make anyone anxious about growing old and penniless.

All your fears about retirement and aging are real. They are challenging to your mental health and quality of life.

Nonetheless, it's important to remember that confronting your fears is your best defense. Knowing what those fears are and then systematically dealing with them by planning your retirement can give you back your power and peace of mind.

There are actions you can take to diminish each of these fears. For example, remaining physically active and leading a healthy lifestyle can reduce your chances of developing illnesses. Kicking bad habits such as smoking and excessive alcohol consumption can improve your physical well-being, thereby minimizing your fear of developing terminal diseases.

Participating in meaningful activities can help you maintain your perspective on your usefulness and can bolster your self-esteem, especially if you pick activities that revolve around your interests and beliefs.

Unlike your preretirement phase of life, when your identity was likely connected to what you did for a living, you are no longer defined by your employment. This change can be a huge relief for many people who were plagued by status-conscious work associates. Now they can contribute to society in other meaningful ways, and enjoy doing it without worrying about how other people see them.

Staying physically active can improve your overall well-being. Weight-bearing exercise and calcium supplements can improve your bone density. These and other "good for you" habits will not only make you feel better and stronger, but will also minimize your concerns about falling and injuring yourself.

Staying engaged with life can help you maintain a positive perspective about your future. Join in with friends, neighbors, and loved ones for social events, volunteer activities, and family get-togethers. People are social creatures, and connecting with society prevents loneliness and helps you stay emotionally healthy.

Be realistic about your fears of retirement. Facing up to and tackling them logically will set you up for a great retirement.

Statistics show that most retirees are living longer and healthier lives than ever before. For most, there's no regret.

The Current Model of Retirement

Retirement isn't what it used to be. It's not as straightforward as it was for our parents. Not only are retirees leaving the workforce earlier in life, they are also staying in retirement longer due to better health and increased longevity. Today's retirees have a different perspective on their ideal lifestyles. They are active, they pursue dreams, they maintain close social ties with their communities, and they emphasize personal growth in their everyday living.

There's a myth out there that most seniors are living in nursing homes. This couldn't be further from the truth. In fact, only about 4 percent of the population at any one time is living in such facilities. Most seniors live in their own homes, with relatives, or in other arrangements within their communities.

What's more, there is also the emerging trend of younger retirees returning to work. In today's world, retirement doesn't necessarily mean a lifestyle of pure leisure. Many retirees are pursuing the work of their choice (as opposed to working from necessity). More and more retirees view a nice blend of part-time employment along with enjoyable leisure activities as the ideal work/life balance for themselves.

Regardless of their reasons, whether they are working out of choice, boredom, or necessity, older workers are becoming the preferred employees for many businesses. Seniors who postpone retirement or return to work part-time after retiring have become the country's retail- and service-sector darlings.

Due to our aging population, a revolution is happening. A new model of retirement is emerging for the baby-boom generation. Retirement today can be as flexible and different from the past as you want it to be.

Changing Needs, Changing Plan

There's no doubt that the key to ensuring you have choice in retirement is financial security, and to achieve financial security, you must stay on top of your financial plan. The main objective of retirement planning is the preservation of your standard of living and the minimization of your chances of running out of money. You may also have other objectives, such as pursuing a hobby or interest, planning for long-term care in your advanced years, and preserving your capital to leave to your heirs.

If you are single, it's important that you start planning now, no matter what your age. The fact is, you have only yourself to rely on. You must realistically budget for your retirement years. Many single seniors are women who are barely making ends meet. Starting to plan as early as possible is crucial for your well-being in retirement.

If you are part of a couple, your finances may be in better shape. You will likely be receiving two income streams while sharing expenses for one household. However, it is incumbent on both of you to communicate your retirement needs and goals to one another. Documenting these wishes can help you avoid misunderstandings later. And even if you are part of a couple now, consider planning also for the eventuality of being single. Undoubtedly, it will happen to either you or your partner at some time.

Regardless of your marital status, planning is crucial to your financial and lifestyle success. Planning must be ongoing for the rest of your life. Retirees need an evolving and flexible money plan. Your needs, spending, and resources change as you age. Your plan must take into account all aspects of your retirement living. For these reasons, planning needs are best examined by breaking down retirement into three distinct phases — active, semi-active, and passive.

Active retirement

This phase of your retirement has more to do with mindset than physiological age. Certainly, for most retirees, it means those years in their lives when they are physically healthy, financially stable, and believe there are still many things to pursue in life and goals that they want to accomplish.

More often than not, active retirees are individuals or couples who are in their early retirement — from their mid-50s to late 60s. They want to travel and see the world, start a dream business, or get involved with legacy or humanitarian projects such as Habitat for Humanities or Oxfam International.

Semi-active retirement

Still mobile and independent in their communities and remaining relatively healthy, retirees at this phase of their lives are likely to slow down the pace of their activities. They are likely to be in their 70s. They have less energy than they used to have, and in the semi-active retirement years, they want to stay closer to home, family, and friends. They want predictability and stability in their daily living. They are less likely to travel far. They are more likely not to be working or be involved in business. Their health is still relatively good, and their interests have now shifted to more gentle activities such as reading, attending regular religious services, or volunteering at a slower pace and closer to home.

Passive retirement

Passive retirees are at a stage in their lives where they've slowed down considerably and may even be experiencing declining health. They're likely to be in their 80s and beyond. Although some of them are still mobile and living independently, they may now be more dependent on others for certain daily living activities such as cleaning house and cooking meals or bathing and dressing.

These retirees will eventually require more than care and assistance in their activities in daily living; they will also need medical and long-term care and attention.

It is expected that more and more passive retirees are going to live beyond the ripe age of 100.

Each of these three stages may bring you different types and/or different mixes of cash inflows (including income and other sources of cash), and you must consider the different expenses that may come your way as you move from one stage to another.

For example, in your active retirement years, you may be one of those seniors who continues or returns to work part-time, and part of your cash inflow may come from this employment. However, that may not be the case as you progress into your passive retirement years, and you must plan ahead for this change in income. It is the same with expenses. You may have a sizeable travel budget during your active retirement, but may completely eliminate this budget item in your passive retirement years.

You need to determine now what you want to do for the rest of your life and plan now how to fund it. You must also determine how you want to live. Depending on your plan, it may be realistic to budget for additional expenses to invest in a hobby or pursue an interest.

As you move into your semi-active retirement years, you may shift your priority to other activities that are closer to home, such as spending more time with families and friends, volunteering with a favorite charity, or becoming more involved with your church or religious organization. This change in activities requires a corresponding shift in your retirement plan to adjust for the new spending pattern.

As you move toward your passive retirement years, your needs will once again change. Your priority will most likely be to make yourself as comfortable and healthy as possible, and this may include extra costs for in-home assistance, medication, and even long-term care. Even if you continue to live in your own home during this phase, alterations to your home may be necessary to accommodate your changing needs. You must consider all these expenses in your overall retirement plan.

Financial Opportunities and Choices

It's a little-known fact, but your early retirement years are the best years to make your investment assets grow. Plan to spend less than your assets can earn for you, and allow the excess return to be reinvested and compounded over time. This strategy is truly careful planning, and it's very wise, too. You will need to draw on these additional resources in your passive retirement years to cover extra care and medical costs.

If you plan to spend less than your income in all your earlier years of retirement, you will be pleasantly surprised by the growth over time by the size of your asset base. Chapter 4 discusses in more detail how you can make your savings grow.

With a little luck and careful planning, your investment assets will have enough time to grow so that they can generate sufficient income to supplement your passive retirement years.

If you find you need additional funds in your passive-retirement years, you may need to convert your non-investment assets into income-generators. If you own your home, here are some options you can consider:

- Add a rental suite for extra income
- Downsize your house to a smaller dwelling to free up cash for investments and paying down debts
- Consider a reverse mortgage to supplement your income stream
- Sell your home outright and rent, and invest the cash from the sale

All phases of retirement require shrewd planning, and it's incumbent on you to make it work. Knowing you have adequate resources to retire for the rest of your life is important.

By putting your goals in writing and getting the numbers down on paper in a budget, you can commit to making your retirement years as carefree as possible. Without a plan, you may be making a leap to financial ruin.

You will find that using this guide to help you budget for all stages of your retirement years can bring you peace of mind about your financial future, and reduce your fear of running out of money in your senior years.

If you are contemplating retirement, take some time to assess your situation. Try the following:

- Complete the necessary worksheets (included online at <www.self-counsel.com/updates/after55/bonus.htm>) to determine your retirement goals and assess your financial situation. Revise your plan where needed to make sure you have adequate resources to cover your retirement.

- List all the advantages you can think of about retiring (e.g., being able to take advantage of last-minute travel specials in off-season periods, or having time to pursue a hobby).

- List all the disadvantages you can think of about retiring (e.g., loss of status or the boredom of having too much time on your hands).

- Compare the two lists. Decide whether the advantages outweigh the disadvantages, or vice versa.

- Discuss retirement with your spouse (if you are part of a couple) to make sure he or she has input into the process and decision.

- Obtain professional help where needed to help you arrive at a logical decision and timeline.

If, after working through all these steps, your gut feeling tells you that you are ready to retire, follow your instinct and do it.

Your retirement years are just beginning. Confront your fears and start living the best years of your life — now!

Chapter 2
YOU CAN DO IT: GOAL SETTING

So let's get started. The first step to enjoying retirement is to identify what your retirement goals are; the next is to put them down on paper. Until you know what you want or need to do in your various retirement phases, you can't adequately plan for your retirement needs.

Issues to Consider

You'll find that many questions come to mind, and you'll need to be aware that the different stages of retirement come with different questions. Here are a few issues you may find yourself considering:

Active retirement years

- How much do I need for retirement living?
- Can I afford to retire?
- How will my retirement plans affect my loved ones?
- What will be my sources of income?
- Where should I live in my retirement years?
- How will I preserve or even grow my capital?

- Have I considered how I might save money after retirement?
- When would I like to retire?
- What would I like to do in my retirement?
- Will I continue working part-time during retirement?
- Will I start a part-time business?
- Do I want to travel? (If yes, to where, for how long, and how often?)
- What hobbies or personal growth would I like to pursue?
- Are there volunteer activities I'd like to pursue?

Semi-active retirement years

- Do I wish to keep my home or sell it and downsize?
- How do I plan to preserve or even improve my health?
- Do I wish to spend more time close to home with family and friends?
- Are there volunteer activities in which I'd like to become involved?
- What household jobs might I hand off to others at this time?
- Would I like to have the option of hiring some household help?

Passive retirement years

- What kind of housing do I think I'll need when this time comes?
- What kinds of activities will I be able to continue to do to keep me involved in life and my community?
- What kind of care or assistance from others do I imagine I'll need?

- Are there other people in my life who might be willing and able to assist me?
- What programs are available through my community or government to make my life easier at this time?
- What legacy do I want to leave behind?

Give some thought to each of these questions, and understand that there may be no simple answers. If you are part of a couple, discuss them with your spouse. Once you've taken some time to consider all aspects of your retirement, you'll be ready to move on to the next step: getting your goals down on paper.

Retirement Goal Setting

Online at <www.self-counsel.com/updates/after55/bonus.htm> you'll find the Retirement Goal Planning worksheet (Worksheet 1). Use this worksheet to list your retirement goals. If you are part of a couple, complete the sheet together. It is a good idea to revisit your goals yearly and revise them where needed.

Take a look at the example of Joe and Martha in Sample 1, at the end of this chapter. Both are in their late 50s. Joe wishes to retire immediately, whereas Martha plans to continue working until she reaches age 62, which will happen in another five years. They are both in good health and are looking forward to a long and fulfilling retirement.

You'll note they've thought through all three stages of their retirement-living years, and that they've included more detail on their worksheet for their earlier years than their later ones. You may find that such is the case for you, too. That's quite acceptable, because your goals may change or evolve over time. You will be identifying your later years' goals now only for reference and general planning purposes. No one can realistically predict what will happen 20 years from now. Just make your best estimate at this time so that you have an idea of what's likely to take place in your future retirement years. Then, make it a point to revisit your goals each year and revise them as needed. Keep in mind also that in addition to changing your goals when it makes sense, you may need to modify your lifestyle to accommodate your new goals.

Making these changes is crucial. You will be developing a financial plan based on your goals. Identifying changes in your goals in advance will allow you to make the corresponding changes to your budget, thereby assuring yourself that you'll continue to successfully fund your retirement. You'll find that doing this alleviates much of the stress associated with retirement, as you'll have the security of knowing that your resources are likely sufficient (barring a catastrophe), no matter what stage of retirement life you're living.

In future chapters, you'll identify where your retirement cash inflows will come from and how much money you can reasonably expect to have. (Remember that cash inflows include any income streams you may have, as well as any cash you may realize from other sources, such as selling your car or cashing in your bonds.) You'll also learn how to make certain your retirement cost is less than your retirement income. This is what is meant by living within your means — the art of living on less than what you bring in.

Once you've identified your retirement goals for the different stages in your retirement years, you'll be ready to take an inventory of where you're at, financially, right now. Calculating your net worth is necessary — and it's the topic of the next chapter.

Sample 1
RETIREMENT GOAL PLANNING

Name(s): ___*Joe (J) & Martha (M)*___

Age: __*(J) 59*__   __*(M) 57*__

Date prepared or revised: __*2004/11/03*__

For active retirement living (first _10_ years):

(M) — continue working full time for 5 years until 62.

(J) — retire immediately.

(J) — 3 to 4 day trips monthly with families and friends.

(J) — prepare family home for sale in 5 years.

(M & J) — relocate and downsize home in 5 years.

(M & J) — extensive traveling in North America after relocation.

(M & J) — plan to exercise, walk, swim 3 times a week

For semi-active retirement living (next _10_ years):

(J & M) — expand home and renovate to accommodate
more visitors.

(J & M) — moderate traveling to visit families and friends.

(J) — take up Psychology noncredit course at local college.

(J & M) — volunteer at their local community center 2 days
a week.

(J & M) — take up Tai Chi or another gentle form of exercise.

For passive retirement living (2nd next _10_ years):

(J & M) — sell home and downsize to appropriate one-
level home or assisted care type facilities.

(J & M) — volunteer where possible and appropriate.

Chapter 3

CALCULATING WHAT YOU ARE WORTH

In dollar terms, how much are you worth today? If you had to make a comparison between your financial situation today and your situation as it will be ten years from now, or as it was one year ago, would you know how to go about doing it? This chapter will take you through a process called the net worth calculation, by which you can answer these questions.

This step is a crucial one, as it helps you to see where you're at financially today. To put it another way, if you sold all your valuables and paid off all your debts now, what would you have left? The amount left is your net worth today.

The calculation serves as an objective starting point by which you can measure your future financial progresses and/or setbacks. Use the Net Worth Worksheet included online at <www.self-counsel.com/updates/after55/bonus.htm> as Worksheet 2 (Sample 2 at the end of this chapter is an example of this worksheet,) to complete your financial snapshot today.

Knowing Your Dollar Value

You can find out what you are worth in dollar terms today simply by taking stock, at fair market value, of everything of value that you own (that is, your assets), and subtracting from that number everything you owe (your liabilities, or debts). The difference is your real worth, or net worth today. A net worth statement shows how well off, financially, you are at a given moment. It not only identifies your assets, but also states their fair market value and the forms in which they exist. Likewise, your liabilities and the nature of these obligations are also identified and valued.

Assets less liabilities equals net worth. For example, if your house on December 31, 2003, is worth $200,000 and has a mortgage balance of $150,000, your net worth at that point in time is $50,000. That's the difference between what you own (the house at $200,000) and what you owe (the mortgage at $150,000).

Now, let's progress a year into the future. You are now valuing your net worth on December 31, 2004. The process is the same, but the values will likely be different. The fair market value of your house may have increased to, say, $225,000. Your mortgage, however, has decreased to $145,000 (due to your diligent payments). Your net worth on December 31, 2004, is $80,000. That's the difference between $225,000 and $145,000. In summary, you've increased your net worth by $30,000 in just one year!

Ideally, your net worth should be growing as you age. To achieve this growth, you must increase your assets and/or decrease your debts. It is a good idea to calculate the change in your net worth at least once every year to measure your progress or setbacks. Depending on your income and spending patterns on retirement, a percentage of your net worth should be used to continuously generate investment income to —

- supplement your retirement living,
- supplement your long-term care,

- grow your net worth,
- leave an estate for your loved ones, and/or
- leave a legacy on death to support your favorite charties, humanitarian agencies, and/or religious organizations.

Running the Numbers

To calculate your own net worth, use the Net Worth Worksheet you'll find online at <www.self-counsel.com/updates/after55/bonus.htm>. Later on, you will use the information from your Net Worth Worksheet when completing the Income-Producing Investments Worksheet, Cash Inflow Worksheet, and Yearly Spending Budget Worksheet, all of which are discussed later in this book. It's a good idea to also revisit these worksheets yearly, re-assess your financial situation, track your financial changes, and make any necessary revisions to your budget and lifestyle.

If you are part of a couple, record both your own and your spouse's assets and liabilities. Any items in both names are recorded as joint assets or liabilities.

If you've never done it before, the following section shows you step by step how to complete your household's own net worth statement. You can make the process fairly painless for yourself by following these steps:

Step 1: Prepare yourself

1. Find a quiet, well-lighted work space.
2. Print out the Net Worth Worksheet form you'll find online at <www.self-counsel.com/updates/after55/bonus.htm>.
3. Have a calculator, a pencil, and an eraser ready for your calculations. (You may choose to complete the *Excel* version of the Net Worth Worksheet available online or print the PDF version and fill in the form by hand.)

4. Gather together the following, if applicable:

- All your most current bank statements.
- All your most current broker and investment account statements.
- All your most current retirement savings account statements.
- All your most current pension account statements.
- All your most current credit card statements.
- All your most current bank, car, and other loan statements.
- All your most current mortgage statements.
- Your life insurance statements, including cash value balances, if any.
- Your long-term care insurance papers.
- Your critical illness insurance papers.
- Your prepaid funeral arrangement papers.
- An itemized listing of your property and valuables with their fair market value. (Separate the listings by type, such as furniture, antiques, jewelry, furs, coin collections, china, crystals, silverware, etc.)

5. Get an accordion-style folder for storing your statements and other papers.

Step 2: Sort out the paperwork

Take a close look at all the papers you have gathered. Sort them into two piles — an "Asset" pile and a "Liability" pile. If you are part of a couple, make additional asset and liability piles for items in your spouse's and joint names.

The "Asset" pile will comprise papers that show the value of the things you own (for example, your investment account statements, the cash value of your life insurance statements, and your itemized listings of valuables). The "Liability" pile will comprise papers that show the value of your debts (for example, your credit card statements, your mortgage statement, and bank statements for overdrawn accounts).

Step 3: Date the Net Worth Worksheet

It is important to record the date for which your net worth was calculated, because when you calculate your net worth again at a future date, you'll be able to make comparisons and measure the progress you've made or any setbacks you've suffered. (You will use this same date again when you fill out the Income-Producing Investments Worksheet.) Note that the date you put on the worksheet is not the actual date on which you did the work; rather, it is the date on which your net worth is based. It is best to pick a date such as December 31, September 30, June 30, or March 31, as these are dates on which most financial institutions provide information on your bank and investment accounts.

Step 4: Fill in the asset values

Complete the "Asset" items and fill in the applicable values on the worksheet, using all available account statements. You may round the values to the nearest one hundred dollars to simplify your calculations.

For items such as your home or your car, for which there are no statements, estimate their fair market value based on your knowledge of the current market and the economy. Fair market value means what you think you can sell them for today. Use the most recent appraised value or, in the case of your home, check with your local realtor. You can use the newspaper's classified section to check for the current value of other assets. You must be realistic, but you don't have to be precise. You will never know the true values of these items until they are actually sold.

In the case of life insurance policies, include only the *cash value* of these policies. Do not include the benefit amount; that will belong to your beneficiaries, not to you.

Step 5: Fill in the liability values

Fill in the amounts of the "Liability" items on the worksheet. Use the values from all available account statements. You may round the values to the nearest one hundred dollars to simplify your calculations.

These are the debts you owe various creditors, including credit card companies and your banks. Don't overlook the debt you may owe to the taxman. (That one should be a top priority in your payment plan.)

Step 6: Fill in the other items/insurance policies

This section itemizes the various insurance policies and their values. Although you pay for these policies, they are not considered assets, because their values are not recognized until certain events occur (such as a particular illness or death), or because they benefit someone else (a beneficiary) and not you. These policies have no current value to you. You simply want to note their existence.

Step 7: Total up your assets

Add up the value of all your assets listed on the worksheet.

Step 8: Total up your liabilities

Add up the value of all your liabilities listed on the worksheet.

Step 9: Calculate your net worth

Subtract the liability total from the asset total. You now know your net worth as of the date you chose in Step 3.

Step 10: File your paperwork

Divide the accordion file into two sections. Label the first half of the file "Assets," and the second half "Liabilities." File your asset-type statements and papers in the "Assets" section, preferably in the same order as you listed them on the Net Worth Worksheet. Do the same with the liability-type statements and papers.

To see how net worth can act as a financial snapshot, look at Sample 2, the completed Net Worth Worksheet of John and Mary as at September 30, 2004. They're both in their early 60s and in good health. Note the following:

1. John has assets of $223,000; Mary has $224,000; and assets in joint names of $437,750. This brings the total household assets to $884,750 as of September 30.

2. Their household liabilities total $28,000.

3. The household net worth is $856,750. That's the difference between total assets and total liabilities.

4. They have bank savings totaling $31,000. The cash in the term deposits and savings is for emergencies. It can be accessed immediately.

5. They have income-producing investments and retirement savings worth $100,750 and $400,000 respectively.

6. They have $30,000 cash value in their life insurance policies. They have named each other and their two grown children as beneficiaries. The cash value will continue to grow over time. They can choose to borrow against it or withdraw the balance at a later time.

7. Their house is worth $250,000, with a remaining mortgage balance of $25,000.

8. They own two vehicles and a recreational vehicle worth $40,000.

9. They have prepaid their respective funeral arrangements.

10. They have purchased critical illness insurance, paying them $50,000 each should they become terminally ill as defined under their policies.

11. John has guaranteed their son John Junior's personal loan of $2,000, which John Junior is expected to repay in full.

Sample 2
NET WORTH WORKSHEET

Net Worth Worksheet of _____ *John & Mary* _____

As At (Date): _____ *2004-09-30* _____

Assets   (what your household owns)

	John	Mary	Joint	Total
Bank				
— Chequing accounts	500	500	1,500	2,500
— Savings accounts			3,500	3,500
— Term deposits			25,000	25,000
— Other savings				
Investments				
— Bonds			30,750	30,750
— Stocks			20,000	20,000
— Mutual funds			40,000	40,000
— Other investments			10,000	10,000
Qualified/ registered retirement acc'ts	200,000	200,000		400,000
Company pensions — cash value				0
Annuities				0
Life insurance — cash value	15,000	15,000		30,000
Prepaid funeral arrangements	5,000	5,000		10,000

Sample 2 — Continued

Real estate					
— Home			250,000	250,000	
— Rental real estate				0	
— Other real estate				0	
Automobiles			20,000	20,000	
RV & boat			20,000	20,000	
Furniture and appliances			15,000	15,000	
Personal valuables					
— Jewelry		2,500		2,500	
— Silverware, china, & stemware			2,000	2,000	
— Collectibles	2,500			2,500	
Other asset items					
Loan to Peter (nephew)		1,000		1,000	
				0	
Total Assets (1)	**$223,000**	**$224,000**	**$437,750**	**$884,750**	

Liabilities   (what your household owes)

	John	Mary	Joint	Total	Interest Rate %
Credit card debt					
— Visa	200	800		1,000	19.0%
— MasterCard			2,000	2,000	18.0%
				0	
Personal loans from bank				0	
Personal loans from others				0	
Car loans				0	
Mortgage			25,000	25,000	7.5%

Income tax debt				0	
Other loans					
				0	
Total Liabilities (2)	**$200**	**$800**	**$27,000**	**$28,000**	

(1) subtract (2)	John	Mary	Joint	Total
Total Assets (1)	223,000	224,000	437,750	884,750
subtract	–	–	–	–
Total Liabilities (2)	200	800	27,000	28,000
equals	=	=	=	=
NET WORTH	$222,800	$223,200	$410,750	$856,750

Other Items / Insurance Policies

Life insurance (John's) — $100,000
  (Beneficiaries — Mary 50%, John Jr. 25%, Tammy Lynn 25%)

Life insurance (Mary's) — $100,000
  (Beneficiaries — John 50%, John Jr. 25%, Tammy Lynn 25%)

Critical illness policy — $50,000 each for John & Mary

Loan guaranteed for John Jr. — $2,000

Grandpa's war medals (cannot ascertain value)

Date prepared: 10/15/2004

They are comforted by the knowledge that —

- they have savings set aside for emergencies, which are sufficient to support them for the next six months;

- they have investments inside and outside their retirement accounts;

- their debts are small and manageable;

- they have insurance coverage (such as property, life, health care and critical illness insurance) to protect themselves against certain unexpected perils; and

- their home can provide them with options for additional income. (These options are discussed in Chapter 8.)

When calculating your own net worth, don't rush. Take your time. You may want to take a break or two, if you need to do so. Remember, your net worth is a financial snapshot of what you're worth as of a particular moment. Keep taking those snapshots, at least once a year, to measure how you are progressing, and assess whether or not your progress is sufficient to fund the kind of retirement you want.

Can you supplement your income from investments and retire? Do you need to work a few years longer? Can you downsize your home and change your net worth snapshot for a better retirement? These and other questions can be answered only after the snapshot is taken.

This process is a crucial one, as it is one of the starting points for planning all phases of your retirement. Use the Net Worth Worksheet to complete your financial snapshot today.

Chapter 4

ASSESSING YOUR INVESTMENTS

How will you fund your retirement? Aside from pension income, you may need your investments and their income to supplement your retirement spending. It's time to take a sober look at what your investments can do for you after you've stopped working. If you have an estimate — ahead of time — of how much money your investments can generate, you'll have a better picture of your retirement finances and can make any necessary changes now, so that you're less likely to worry about your future.

So far, you made a list of your retirement goals and you've taken stock of what you own and owe by completing your Net Worth Worksheet. You are now ready to complete the Income-Producing Investments Worksheet to determine how much income your assets can likely make for you. It also guides you to calculate how much cash you can expect to withdraw from your investments for daily living.

It's imperative to your financial well-being that you determine whether or not your investments are right for you. Are they producing enough income, cash inflow, and overall return based on your risk-tolerance level? The exercise set out in this chapter will give you the information you need to make your decisions.

What kind of investor are you? Are you afraid of taking risks? Or can you go on a roller-coaster ride with your hard-earned dollars and still sleep soundly at night? The conventional rule is, the more risk you take on, the greater the return you can expect. Do keep in mind, however, that this is your savings to fund your retirement. Gambling it all (for all or nothing) is not recommended.

If you are a risk taker, you should still fund a good portion of your savings in conservative, stable, and income-generating investments. They provide the base of income to support your retirement years, even if your riskier investments drop in value or stop paying you an income stream.

The secret to successful investing on retirement is to strike an appropriate balance between the various types of investments: some should be lower risk, some higher risk, and some in between. It is not recommended that you time the market (a process by which you pick the right time to move your investments in and out of the markets in hopes of earning a higher return). Timing the market can be risky and is not recommended for the bulk of your investment portfolio. Generally speaking, the older you are, the less risk you should take with your investments. You do not want to gamble with your retirement money.

You also want to ensure that your investments are balanced between investments inside and outside your qualified or registered retirement accounts. It is also important, for income and estate-tax considerations, to pay attention to the type of qualified retirement accounts you hold (for example, a US traditional IRA or a Roth IRA). There are myriad plans to consider, and each one has its own unique features, benefits, and limitations.

Tax issues can be extremely complicated and specific to location, and so fall outside the scope of this book. You must plan for your own situation very carefully, depending on your jurisdiction and financial circumstances. To maximize your unique tax-advantaged investment mix, you should work with a certified financial planner or tax professional in your area.

ABC's of Investing: Common Types of Investments

Safety investments

Safety investments are generally available in US and Canadian dollars. They are relatively short-term — usually less than one year to maturity. They are issued by financial institutions and governments. Safety investments include —

- savings accounts with your financial institution,
- short-term certificates of deposit,
- short-term treasury bills, and
- money-market mutual funds.

Safety investments are considered safe because they usually offer you a certain rate of interest and are guaranteed by the financial institution or the government. They can be cashed fairly quickly, and there's very little risk of you not getting your money back.

But these investments also offer you the lowest rates of return. They are ideal instruments for you to use if you need to park your money somewhere temporarily. For example, you've got a few thousand dollars in your checking account, and you don't need to use this money for bill payments for another month. You may want to transfer this cash into a money-market fund and earn some interest on it while it's sitting idle. You transfer the money back into your checking account when it's time to use it for bill payments.

Money-market mutual funds are pools of very short-term investments in which you can participate anytime. They are highly liquid, meaning you can transfer your money in and out of these funds very quickly. Most of these funds require only one day's notice to cash them in and out. You will earn interest for the time your money is in the pool.

Income investments

Income-type investments earn interest income. In essence, you loan your money to governments, financial institutions, or corporations for a period of usually 5 to 20 years. In return for the use of your money, the borrowers promise to pay back the loan to you on a stated date and also promise to pay you regular interest. Because of the additional risk you take on in this type of investment, the interest rates they pay you are higher than those associated with the safety-type investments. Common income-type investments include —

- government bonds,
- guaranteed investment certificates (GICs),
- term deposits, and
- corporate bonds.

Another type of income investment is dividend income-producing preferred stocks. Preferred stocks are a special class of ownership of a corporation. They are usually issued by large and well-established corporations, called blue-chip corporations. Preferred stocks carry no voting rights but may come with special features, such as options for bond conversions and cumulative unpaid dividend income.

Dividend income is your share of the authorized distribution of the corporation's profit. Many investors buy preferred stocks for their regular payment of dividend income, and these investments are also viewed as being more secure because they are usually issued by blue-chip corporations. In addition, when you sell preferred stocks, you'll have either capital gains or losses, depending on whether you made or lost money on the transactions.

Growth investments

The most common growth-type investments are common stocks and preferred stocks (which were touched on in the previous section).

Preferred stockholders rank ahead of common stockholders in claims on the corporation's assets, which becomes important if the company in which the stock is held fails.

Common stocks represent partial ownership in a corporation. Most common stockholders have voting rights. However, should the corporation fail, common stockholders rank last in being paid, behind creditors, bondholders, and preferred stockholders (in that order). There are other risks associated with owning common stocks, but investors expect a higher rate of return for investing in them.

There are different types of common stocks:

1. *Blue-chip stocks.* These are described in the previous section.

2. *Growth stocks.* These are common stocks of corporations that have potential for huge growth over time. Such stocks usually offer potential for attractive capital gains but offer no dividends, because these corporations may not be in a profitable position yet or are investing their profits back into their operations.

Growth stocks are considered risky investments. You may "make a killing" if the corporation is successful, but you can also lose it all if the corporation folds. Stocks of start-up mining, high-tech, and bio-tech corporations are examples of growth stocks.

Mutual funds

Mutual funds are investments you buy to become a stakeholder in a pool or basket of professionally managed stocks or bonds, or a combination of both. Over the years, mutual funds have become very popular with investors. Today, there are literally hundreds of mutual funds to choose from. They are sold in units, and normally the price per unit fluctuates depending on the underlying fair market value of the stocks and bonds. Usually you can buy and sell these units on the open market, just as you do with stocks.

You can buy any stock or bond, as well as other things, through a mutual fund. Professionally managed mutual funds include —

- short- and long-term government and corporate bonds,
- mortgages,
- treasury bills,
- preferred stocks,
- growth stocks,
- foreign government and corporate bonds, and
- foreign stocks (of many countries around the world).

The following are common types of mutual funds:

- *Bond funds:* mutual funds that invest in a variety of bonds.
- *Equity funds:* mutual funds that invest in a variety of stocks.
- *Balanced funds:* mutual funds that invest in a combination of stocks and bonds.
- *Foreign funds:* mutual funds that invest in other countries' stocks and bonds.

There are many different funds, fund types, and fund companies to choose from. The funds vary greatly by the type of investments they hold. They range from holding very conservative investments to Las Vegas style, roll-of-the-dice risky investments. You must understand the nature of the funds you are buying before buying them. Always read the prospectuses of the funds you're interested in and make sure they fit in with the rest of your portfolio, your investment style, and risk-tolerance level.

Real property investment

It is appropriate and prudent to add real estate to your investment portfolio, especially if your portfolio is of a sizeable amount. It is not advisable to hold only real estate in your investment portfolio. Rather, it should be part of your total investment package, which should include other investments such as bonds, stocks, mutual funds, and the like. This helps to better diversify your investments and spread out your investment risk. Your principal residence is excluded as a real property investment.

Many investors with a long-term view and patience have been rewarded with sizeable gains when they finally sell their properties. During their period of property holding, some even manage to profit from renting their holdings out, and take advantage of tax deductions to generate even more cash.

No question, real estate offers retirees a potential stream of cash inflow in the form of rental income. However, it also has its unique considerations. Many retirees do not wish to become landlords. Managing a rental property is no easy feat, especially if you are unlucky enough to inherit troublesome tenants. Nonetheless, it can be worthwhile for those who are willing to take on the risk of long-term real property investment.

Being Wise

You can see there are many different investment products from which to choose. Always keep in mind that if you desire a higher rate of return, you must expect to take on more risk. With higher-risk investments, you must be prepared for the possibility that you can lose part or all of your investment.

Ensuring the safety of your capital should be a priority when you are investing during your retirement years. The key to successful retirement investing lies in finding your comfort level between risk and return, while still generating enough income to support your lifestyle.

Always do your homework before you invest. If necessary, seek out professional advice.

Here are some sensible tips for retirement investing:

1. *Don't be greedy with investment returns.* Strive for an adequate return to supplement and maintain your

Chart 1
SAVINGS CHART SUMMARY GUIDE

Savings Chart Summary Guide
Cumulative Saving Factors

Value per: $1.00
Interest rate: various

After	return @ 3%	return @ 4%	return @ 5%	return @ 6%	return @ 7%	return @ 8%	return @ 9%	return@ 10%	return @ 12%
5 years	1.159	1.217	1.276	1.338	1.403	1.469	1.539	1.611	1.762
10 years	1.344	1.480	1.629	1.791	1.967	2.159	2.367	2.594	3.106
15 years	1.558	1.801	2.079	2.397	2.759	3.172	3.642	4.177	5.474
20 years	1.806	2.191	2.653	3.207	3.870	4.661	5.604	6.727	9.646
25 years	2.094	2.666	3.386	4.292	5.427	6.848	8.623	10.835	17.000
30 years	2.427	3.243	4.322	5.743	7.612	10.063	13.268	17.449	29.960
35 years	2.814	3.946	5.516	7.686	10.677	14.785	20.414	28.102	52.800
40 years	3.262	4.801	7.040	10.286	14.974	21.725	31.409	45.259	93.051

The above chart assumes a perfect return environment from year to year as indicated. It is provided as a guide only. Your actual return factor may differ.

of inconsistent returns from year to year. Nonetheless, it is a guideline to give you a sense of what you can achieve with your investments over time when you allow them to grow through reinvestment.

Let's assume you have $100,000 in your qualified or registered retirement account at age 55. You expect to earn a 6 percent return on this account and will not be withdrawing from it until age 65. The chart shows that if everything goes as planned, your $100,000 will grow to $179,100 ($100,000 x factor 1.791). That's an increase of $79,100! If you can leave it intact until age 70 (that is, for 15 years), the plan will grow to $239,700 ($100,000 x factor 2.397)! You will earn an additional $60,000 just by leaving the account alone for five more years.

You can see that the longer you leave the money reinvested, the larger the factor and the bigger your resulting nest egg. Even when you need to withdraw funds from your account, compounding can still continue as long as the amount you withdraw is less than the expected rate of return on the account.

For example, say that you expect to earn 8 percent return on your investments, but reinvest only 3 percent (withdrawing the difference of 5 percent). On a $100,000 investment, the account will grow to $134,400 in ten years' time ($100,000 x 1.344 factor).

What Will Your Investments Produce for You?

The following exercise shows you how to assess your own investments and estimate their income. For this exercise, you will complete the Income-Producing Investments Worksheet (Worksheet 3) included online at <www.self-counsel.com /updates/after55/bonus.htm>. You can make the process fairly painless for yourself by following these steps:

Step 1: Prepare yourself

1. Find a quiet, well-lighted work space.

2. Have your completed Net Worth Worksheet at hand.

3. Print out the Income-Producing Investments form that you will find online.

4. Have a calculator, a pencil, and an eraser ready to make your calculations. (You may choose to complete the *Excel* version of the Income-Producing Investments Worksheet.)

5. Gather the following:

   • All your most current bank statements.

   • All your most current broker and investment account statements.

   • All your most current retirement savings account statements.

   • All information on other income-generating assets such as rental properties, IOUs, etc.

Step 2: Date the Income-Producing Investments Worksheet

It is important to record the date for which your investment income was calculated. By doing so, you'll be able to make comparisons and measure progress or setbacks when you calculate your projected returns again at a future date.

Note that the date you put on the worksheet is not the actual date on which you did the work (that's on page 2); rather, it is the date on which your investments are valuated. It's best to pick a date such as December 31, June 30, or March 31, as these are the dates most commonly used by financial institutions and governments when they produce statements of your accounts. This date should be the same as the date on your Net Worth Worksheet.

Step 3: Transfer information from your Net Worth Worksheet

Copy all income-producing asset values from the Asset section of the Net Worth Worksheet to the corresponding lines on page 1 of the Income-Producing Investments Worksheet. These will include bank saving accounts, term deposits, bonds, stocks, mutual funds, qualified or registered retirement accounts, rental properties, etc.

Step 4: Fill in the Income-Producing Investment items

On page 2 of the Income-Producing Investments Worksheet, list the items that make up the total of each line on page 1. A reference letter is assigned to each type of asset: A for banks, B for bonds, C for stocks, etc.

Complete all detailed asset items and fill in the applicable values and other relevant information on page 2 of the worksheet. Refer to all the available account statements at your disposal. You may round the values to the nearest one hundred dollars to simplify your calculations.

Step 5: Estimate the income for each investment

Continue working with page 2, closely reviewing your investment statements and other documents, and estimating the expected income to be earned from each investment for the year. Record this estimate for each asset in the yearly income column on the same line as the asset is listed. For example, a $10,000 GIC for one year guaranteeing you 2.5 percent in interest should earn you $250 in yearly income.

For investments such as stocks and mutual funds, you may have to estimate their dividend and other incomes based on historical and previous years' returns. This information is available from your previous years' investment statements, the Internet, or estimates from your advisors and brokers.

Do not include unrealized gains (gains from investments that have not been sold but have appreciated in value) as income. These gains will be recognized indirectly (as cash inflows) when these assets are sold.

For qualified or registered retirement accounts, estimate both the expected returns and yearly withdrawals in the appropriate columns. These can be different numbers. You may withdraw from the account what's required by law or according to your needs, rather than the amount the account earns. If there is a surplus, the difference is what is reinvested in the account. If there is a shortfall, the value of the account for next year will decrease.

Step 6: Estimate other income

If you have other sources of income such as rental income, estimate them net of their related expenses. List the applicable information in the Other Investments section.

Step 7: Total all sections on page 2 and record the prepared date on the worksheet

Total each investment section on page 2 as determined in Steps 5 and 6. Grand total all sections' investment income in the Total Income box. Complete the Date Prepared box at the bottom of the worksheet.

Step 8: Transfer the investments and inflow totals

Transfer the Total Income and Total Yearly Retirement Account Withdrawal Amounts to the applicable lines on the Cash Inflow Worksheet. Instructions for completing this worksheet will be discussed in Chapter 5.

Step 9: File your paperwork

File the reviewed papers in the accordion file under Assets.

Have a look at Sample 3, which is the completed Income-Producing Investments Worksheet for John and Mary. Note the following:

1. John and Mary's income-producing investments are in joint names.

2. The value of their qualified retirement saving accounts is fairly evenly split. (Income splitting is usually a good tax-saving strategy.)

3. The yearly investment income is estimated at $5,288.

4. For now, they choose to withdraw from their qualified retirement accounts $10,000, an amount less than the estimated return of $30,000. This move enables them to grow their retirement saving accounts, tax free, until the money is needed in later years.

5. Their savings of $28,500 is their emergency money. The GIC is cashable after 90 days.

6. Investments in mutual funds, both inside and outside their qualified retirement accounts, are well diversified between bond, equity, balanced, and foreign investments, with emphasis on safety of capital. They choose to hold conservative investments because of their retirement age. They have also chosen only reputable and large mutual-fund companies for their investments.

7. They hold Bank of America stocks for their steady dividend income stream and blue-chip-stock status.

John and Mary are comfortable with their conservative investment style. They know that in all likelihood, their capital is preserved and has a modest potential for growth.

Now that the numbers are all on paper, they can see that they are not withdrawing and spending all their investment returns. They are reinvesting the excess income, tax free, in their respective retirement savings accounts.

For now, they are happy with the plan as written. They will increase their retirement account withdrawal rate as required by law over the next ten years and as their care needs increase. They will closely monitor the accounts' growth yearly.

They also plan on engaging a tax professional and/or a certified financial planner to help them maximize their tax savings and prepare for proper estate planning. Because they have inventoried all their investments and documented their estimated returns, their tax-planning process is that much more simple and organized.

Sample 3
INCOME-PRODUCING INVESTMENTS

Income-Producing Investments

Worksheet of __John & Mary__

As At (Date): __2004/09/30__

Assets (what your household owns)

	Reference for details	John (J)	Mary (M)	Joint (Jnt)	Total
Bank					
— Savings accounts	A			3,500	3,500
— Term deposits / GICs	A			25,000	25,000
— Other savings	A				0
Investments					
— Bonds	B			30,750	30,750
— Stocks	C			20,000	20,000
— Mutual funds	E			40,000	40,000
— Other investments	G			10,000	10,000
Qualified retirement accounts	F	200,000	200,000		400,000
Real estate —					
— Rental real estate	G				0
— Other real estate	G				
Other asset items					
	G				0
	G				0
	G				0

Sample 3 — Continued

A — Term Deposits & Guaranteed Investment Certificates (GICs) *(estimated)*

Description /Financial Instit'n	Principal $	Interest rate	Term	Expiry date	Yearly income
ING bank 1-year term, cashable after 90 days	20,000	2.5%	1 year	7/31/2005	500
Coastal S & L 2-year GIC	5,000	2.6%	2 years	4/30/2006	130
Savings acc't	3,500	0.5%			18
Total term deposits & GICs	**$28,500**				**$648**

B — Bonds *(estimated)*

Description of instruments	Face value	Purchase price	Interest rate	Maturity date	Fair mkt value	Yearly income
GMC corporate — 10-year bond	30,000	30,250	4.5%	12/31/2010	30,750	1,350
Total bonds	**$30,000**				**$30,750**	**$1,350**

Sample 3 — Continued

C — Stocks *(estimated)*

Description of shares	Purchase date	# of shares	Total cost	Fair mkt value	Yearly dividends
IBE	2003	100	5,500	7,800	0
Bank of America	2002	100	10,000	12,200	860
Total stocks				**$20,000**	**$860**

E — Mutual Funds *(estimated)*

Description of funds	Purchase date	# of units	Total cost	Fair mkt value	Yearly income
Johnson S/T bond	2003	200	4,000	4,500	300
Hager Bidwell Small Cap	2002	100	3,000	4,000	100
Hager Bidwell Large Cap	2000	100	5,000	3,500	210
Vanduez Cdn	2002	50	1,500	2,200	150
Vanduez Asia Pac	1999	50	2,500	1,800	50
Vanduez European	1999	50	2,500	2,000	120
Great Alta Balanced	2000	400	20,000	22,000	1,000
			$38,500	**$40,000**	**$1,930**

Sample 3 — Continued

G — Other Investments *(estimated)*

Description of investment	Purchase date	# of units	Total cost	Fair mkt value	Yearly income
Private investment — Uncle Phil's Deli	2003	10,000	10,000	10,000	500
			$10,000	$10,000	$500

Total income	$5,288

To cash inflow worksheet

F — Qualified or Registered Retirement Accounts *(estimated)*

Description of account		Fair mkt Value	(Estimated) Yearly return		Yearly withdrw'l
John's retirement acc't		200,000	15,000		5,000
Mary's retirement acc't		200,000	15,000		5,000
		$400,000	$30,000		$10,000

To cash inflow worksheet

Date prepared: 10/15/2004

Chapter 5
SHOW ME THE MONEY

After completing the Net Worth Worksheet and the Income-Producing Investments Worksheet, you will be ready to determine how much money will be available to you from all sources during your retirement. During your preretirement years, when you are employed or self-employed, your income from your work is your main source of cash inflow. However, retirement income is an entirely different stream. This chapter can help you identify potential sources of cash inflow for your post-working life.

From Where Will the Money Flow?

For most retirees, there are four main sources of retirement income: government benefits, company-pension benefits, personal retirement savings withdrawals, and your personal investments. To discover how much money you may expect to have, factor in the total amount you can expect to receive from each source every year. Add to this number the amount of money you expect to realize from supplementary income from such sources as part-time employment, self-employment, and/or rental income. You must make sure the total income from all sources is sufficient to support the day-to-day retirement lifestyle you have in mind, especially during your active and semi-active retirement years. If it isn't, you may have to adjust your expectations. (For instance, you may have to consider delaying your retirement or you may have to reduce your retirement spending.) It is not a good idea to draw from your capital to supplement your day-to-day living, unless you've planned for this withdrawal when you reach your passive retirement years.

Running the Numbers

Two different Cash Inflow Worksheets are provided online at <www.self-counsel.com/updates/after55/bonus.htm> to help you make your estimate: the Cash Inflow Worksheet for Active and Semi-Active Retirees (Worksheet 4), and the Cash Inflow Worksheet for Passive Retirees (Worksheet 5) to cover the three different phases of retirement living. Choose the worksheet that covers the phase of retirement for which you are making your plans. If you are still working, you'll most likely be completing the Cash Inflow Worksheet for Active or Semi-Active Retirees. If you are already retired and are contemplating moving from active to semi-active retirement, you'll also most likely be completing the same worksheet. However, if you and/or your spouse are in your advanced retirement years or have reached a point at which you are contemplating assisted living or long-term care, the Cash Inflow Worksheet for Passive Retirees is the one you'll need to complete now.

The difference between the two worksheets is the inclusion of active income in the Cash Inflow Worksheet for Active and Semi-Active Retirees; while the emphasis is placed on possible capital withdrawals in the Cash Inflow Worksheet for Passive Retirees.

It is more likely you'll have some active income to supplement your retirement while you are in your active and semi-active years. You will be completely relying on your pension and investment income during your passive retirement years, and be looking to capital withdrawals for any additional assisted or long-term care expenses. That's why it's desirable to avoid making any capital withdrawals from your investments for as long as possible.

Regardless of which Cash Inflow Worksheet you choose, you must complete it in detail. Please note that cash inflow is different from income. Cash inflow takes into account non-income cash, such as the money you may get from selling your car or from selling your mutual funds.

These sheets are a straightforward list of potential sources of cash for you, or for you and your spouse if you are part of a couple. The purpose of the exercise of filling them out is to help you budget and live within your means, no matter what phase of your retirement life you're planning.

If you are single, list all your potential sources of cash inflow in the first of the three columns, add them up, and enter the total on the line "Total before-tax cash inflow." If you are part of a couple, list your cash inflow sources in the first of the three columns, and your spouse's in the middle column. Go across line by line, adding your and your spouse's numbers together, and enter the total for each line in the last of the three columns. Once you have done this, add up all the numbers in that column (marked "Total"), and enter the sum on the line "Total before-tax cash inflow."

Be certain you have identified all sources of retirement cash inflow available to you. You will also need to estimate the income taxes you must pay for the year. (Please note that income taxes can vary widely between jurisdictions. Do your homework or consult a professional accountant to make certain your income tax estimate is realistic.) Enter your estimated income taxes on the line "Less: Estimated income taxes." What remains when you subtract your estimated income taxes from your total cash inflow is the net cash available to you for your retirement living. This is the amount you can spend.

You'll need to continue filling out the worksheet applicable to your situation every year. Tracking your sources of cash inflow will help you create a realistic budget for yourself. You can anticipate changes to your lifestyle before they become necessary and be ready to make them when the time comes.

Sources of Cash Inflow

What follows below is a brief discussion of certain benefits you may be eligible for upon retirement. You will have to check with your employer, government, or veterans' group to determine whether or not you qualify. Alternatively, a certified financial planner may be able to help you.

Company pensions

Some employers provide pension money for their retired employees. If you are fortunate enough to belong to a company pension plan, make yourself thoroughly familiar with it. As a crucial part of your retirement-planning process, find out what options are available to you, how much money you can expect to receive from the plan, and thoroughly understand all restrictions and limitations you are accepting before signing off on the paperwork. It is recommended you use the service of a qualified pension professional if the choices are varied and complicated. You want to make sure you are picking the best option available to you.

In all likelihood, if you accept early retirement from your company, you'll receive smaller monthly pension payments than you would if you wait until you reach full retirement age. Make sure you know what the limits are and determine for yourself if early retirement is for you. Be sure to get an answer also on whether or not your employer will provide you with continued health care coverage if you retire early. You may find that if you have no coverage (us only) before Medicare kicks in at age 65, depending on your jurisdiction, the cost to cover yourself may be too prohibitive for you to even think about retiring.

Qualified or registered retirement accounts

These are government registered saving accounts you've set up during your working years to save for your own and/or your spouse's retirement. Depending on your age, you may or must withdraw a certain amount from your qualified or registered retirement account each year. Also depending on your jurisdiction, the amount of withdrawal may or may not be taxable. For example, a traditional IRA (or a Canadian RRSP or RRIF) withdrawal is taxable, whereas a withdrawal from a Roth IRA is not.

Be cautious of restrictions. There may be penalties for early withdrawals, just as there are for non-withdrawals when you reach a certain age. You must do your planning homework as early as possible. To make the process easier, you may wish to seek the help of a certified financial planner to make certain that your withdrawal process is right for you.

International social security agreement pensions

You may be entitled to receive a reciprocal social security/ pension payment if you have worked in another country and contributed to its government pension plan. The United States, Canada, and numerous other countries have similar reciprocal agreements. Check with your local federal government pension office for details to see if you and/or your spouse qualify. The following websites may provide some useful information:

- US: Social Security Administration (International Benefits) <www.ssa.gov/international>
- Canada: Social Development Canada (International Benefits) <www.sdc.gc.ca>

Social Security benefits (US)

Social Security is a government benefit payable on retirement. The amount of the benefit you may receive depends on your average earnings over most of your working life. If you are taking Social Security at the earliest eligible age (62) instead of your full-benefit age (currently between 65 and 67, depending on your year of birth), you will take a 20 percent to 30 percent reduction in monthly payments. The closer you are to your full-benefit age, the smaller the reduction.

Be wary of the steep penalty levied against earned income while you're receiving social security benefits, especially if you retire early (when the stipulated maximum annual limit of what you can earn is low) but decide to return to work part-time. The penalty can be as great as $1 for every $2 earned. You may be better off if you delay receiving Social Security benefits until you reach your full retirement age.

Survivor benefits may be available to widows/widowers through Social Security. If you lose your spouse, you should apply immediately.

Check with your local office of the Social Security Administration or visit their website <www.ssa.gov> for more details.

Veterans benefit payments (US)

You may be eligible for Veterans Affairs (VA) benefits if you are a veteran. The major benefit categories available to veterans include the following:

- Disability
- Health care
- Dependents' and survivors' benefits
- Education and training
- Life insurance

Check with your local US Department of Veterans Affairs office or visit their website for more details. Ask for the brochure titled *Summary of VA Benefits*. See the Resources section at the back of this book for contact information.

Canada Pension Plan (CPP) payments (Canada)

CPP is a government-administered pension benefit plan payable to retirees aged 60 or older. The amount of the pension payable is dependent on the contributions you make to the plan over most of your working years. If you opt to begin taking early CPP payments at age 60 instead of at the full retirement age of 65, you may find you are forced to take a cut in your monthly payments of up to 30 percent.

CPP may also pay out survivor benefits to the spouse or partner of a deceased person. If you lose your spouse, you should apply for these benefits immediately.

For more details, check with Social Development Canada or visit their website <www.sdc.gc.ca>. See the Resources section of this book.

Old Age Security (OAS) payments (Canada)

OAS is a universal benefit available to Canadian seniors aged 65 and older. You must apply for OAS before you can begin to receive this benefit. However, be aware that it is subject to a government clawback of the benefit if your income exceeds a certain amount annually (currently set at approximately $58,000).

Once again, for more details, check with Social Development Canada or visit their website <www.sdc.gc.ca>. See the Resources section of this book.

Veteran's benefits (Canada)

If you are a veteran of the Canadian Armed Forces, you may qualify for various benefit programs. The categories of benefits available to veterans include the following:

- Disability
- Prisoner-of-war compensation
- Income-tested benefits
- Merchant-navy veterans benefits

- Health and residential care
- Survivor benefits

Check with your local Canadian Veterans Affairs office or visit their website for more details. See the Resources section at the back of this book for more information.

Other Income-Generating Options

In addition to receiving any benefits for which you may be eligible, you may also be able to generate income in other ways. Consider the options discussed below.

Returning to work part-time

You may choose to return to the workforce on a part-time or seasonal basis. You may wish to supplement your pension income, to re-connect with people, to update your skills, or maybe your motivation includes all three of these desires.

Regardless of your reasons, there are numerous part-time employment opportunities for retirees today. Many companies are beginning to recognize the benefits of hiring older workers. Those older than age 65 already have regular health benefits through Medicare and are also receiving Social Security income. These features make them more attractive to employers, as they know these workers are not completely dependent on their employment income for day-to-day living.

Because businesses are now beginning to consider older workers desirable, opportunities are opening up for seniors. As more and more seniors choose to work, it becomes more acceptable for people to work beyond the usual retirement age. More options in employment are becoming available, and employers will likely become more willing to accommodate older workers' need to work shorter and irregular shifts.

The upside for business is real. Senior employees are less demanding than many of their younger counterparts. There is less turnover among senior employees, they are more patient with customers, and are, on the whole, more reliable in their commitment to the job. According to the US Bureau of Labor Statistics, workers older than 55 are the fastest-growing segment of the country's labor force. By 2010, the agency estimates that almost 27 million Americans older than 55 will be working — a 46 percent increase since 2000.

What would you be interested in doing? Give yourself some breathing space to find suitable part-time employment. If your preretirement work left you feeling burned out, you should definitely avoid the same type of work. Consider your skills, knowledge, and personality. Throw in a bit of fun and an element of challenge. That's what your post-retirement job should look like.

There is one caution that must be mentioned. Look closely at the impact of earned income on your social security benefits, especially if you are in early retirement. As mentioned above, you may lose as much as $1 in benefits for every $2 you earn.

Check with your local office of the Social Security Administration or visit their website <www.ssa.gov> for more details.

Home-based business income

Have you ever considered starting and running your own business, but just never had the time? Retirement can make it possible. There are plenty of part-time businesses that are suitable for retirees. Not only can you start a business to earn extra income, you can also run it out of your home and thereby fit it easily into your retirement lifestyle.

The key is to find the business that is right for you. Here are only a few of the hundreds of businesses you might find suitable:

- Tutoring
- Temping and holiday replacement service
- Consulting
- Bed and breakfast

- Floral arrangements
- Catering
- Tour guiding
- Graphics design
- Custom tailor and alterations
- Custom gift baskets
- Personal chef
- Desktop publishing
- Freelance writing
- Bookkeeping
- Word processing
- Artistic pursuits (e.g., painting, pottery making, sculpting, etc.)
- Delivery service
- Carpentry
- Electrical and electronic repairs
- Web design and support services

When thinking about starting a business, however, there are a few questions you must ask yourself before plunging ahead. Consider the following:

- Will you enjoy it?
- Can you afford it?
- Is it easy to learn?
- Will it be manageable and easy to run?
- Does your municipality allow it to be operated from home?
- Does your residential-apartment/condominium complex allow it to be operated from home?
- Do you qualify to take out extra insurance coverage for your home business?

- Will it jeopardize your health?
- Will it infringe too much on your retirement lifestyle?

Again, you must carefully consider the impact the extra income may have on your social security benefits, as discussed above.

Rental income from your home

Another potential source of cash inflow can be realized by renting out part of your home. It's worth considering if you have an extra room or a finished basement suite available. It is especially ideal if your home is located close to a college, university, or hospital. College and university students and hospital workers may all be potential renters.

Take the time to find the right tenant. You'll not only gain an extra source of income, but may also benefit from having a reliable housesitter when you decide to travel!

An example

Take a look at Sample 4, the completed Cash Inflow Worksheet for Bob and Jane, another hypothetical couple contemplating retirement.

They're both 56, healthy, and active, so they've completed the Cash Inflow Worksheet for Active Retirees. Note the following:

- Their before-tax income from all sources totals $52,900.

- Their after-tax income for living expenses is estimated at $44,900.

- Jane wishes to continue working part-time at the local community center, while Bob works part-time for a cruise ship company during the busy season.

- For now, they are actively growing their qualified retirement accounts by reinvesting the income. By doing this, they are building up their nest egg and will be able to cover the extra care they anticipate needing when they move into passive retirement.

- Note that Bob and Jane have also — quite wisely — completed the Cash Inflow Worksheet for Passive Retirees (see Sample 5). They want a rough estimate of their cash inflow in their passive retirement years, although they are still some 20 years away.

- The next step for them is to complete the Yearly Spending Budget Worksheet for Active Retirees, to determine what spending needs they will have as active retirees. They hope that a simplified lifestyle in retirement will enable them to live within their means.

- The next chapter, Yearly Retirement Spending Budget, will help you create a budget to help you ensure that you keep your expenses within the limits of your total cash inflow.

Sample 4
CASH INFLOW WORKSHEET
(For active & semi-active retirees)

Cash Inflow Worksheet of _Bob & Jane_
For the year _2005_
(For active and semi-active retirees)

Income Sources: Single or Couple Total	Bob	Jane	Total
Company pensions	22,000	18,000	40,000
Qualified or registered retirement account withdrawals (from *Income-Producing Investments Worksheet*)	0	0	0
Government pensions	0	0	0
Other pensions & annuity payments			
Investment cash inflow (from *Income-Producing Investments Worksheet*)	3,000	3,000	6,000
Part-time employment income	2,400	4,500	6,900
Self-employment income			
Other active income			
Sale of assets (bonds, stocks, real properties, vehicles, etc.)			
Other cash sources			
Total before tax cash inflow	**$27,400**	**$25,500**	**$52,900**
Less: estimated income taxes (*)	4,100	3,900	8,000
Total income	**$23,300**	**$21,600**	**$44,900**

to Yearly Spending Budget Worksheet

(*) Your actual taxes will vary, depending on your jurisdiction and other tax-related variables.

Sample 5
CASH INFLOW WORKSHEET
(For passive retirees)

Cash Inflow Worksheet of ___*Bob & Jane*___
For the year ___*2005*___
(For passive retirees)

Income Sources: Single or Couple Total	Bob	Jane	Total
Company pensions	22,000	18,000	40,000
Qualified or registered retirement account withdrawal (from *Income-Producing Investments Worksheet*) (***)	10,000	10,000	20,000
Government pensions	10,000	8,500	18,500
Other pensions & annuity payments			
Investment cash inflow (from *Income-Producing Investments Worksheet*)	5,500	5,500	11,000
Sale of assets (bonds, stocks, real properties, vehicles, etc.) sold $10,000 in mutual funds (**)	5,000	5,000	10,000
Other cash sources			
Total before tax cash inflow	52,500	47,000	99,500
Less: estimated income taxes (*)	$10,000	$8,500	$18,500
Total after tax cash inflow	42,500	38,500	81,000

(*) Your actual taxes will vary, depending on your jurisdiction and other tax-related variables.

(**) Only capital gain portion may be taxable.

(***) Amount withdrawn for cash inflow purpose may be less than required withdrawal amount. Difference is assumed reinvested for income.

Chapter 6

YEARLY RETIREMENT SPENDING BUDGET

It's to your advantage to create a budget for each stage of your retirement years. Whether you are in active, semi-active, or passive retirement, you must know that you have adequate financial resources. The further ahead you plan, the better off you'll be. This chapter can help you judge what your spending needs may be so that you can work out a budget for yourself.

By now, you will have completed the Net Worth Worksheet, so you know, in dollar terms, how much you are worth. You will also have filled out the Income-Producing Investments Worksheet, which shows you how much cash your investments, savings, and qualified or registered retirement accounts can generate for you. Your Cash Inflow Worksheet shows you how much money you can expect to have to live on. Now it is time for the next step: estimating your spending.

Your Expenses

What follows here is a list of the more common spending categories you need to think about and include in your budget for all stages of your retirement. *(Please note that not every category will apply to you at every stage of your retirement.)*

- Housing costs: basic
- Housing costs: in-home care
- Housing costs: assisted-living facility
- Housing costs: long-term care facility
- Housing cost credits: insurance coverage or other subsidies
- Utilities
- Food and sundries
- Transportation
- Various insurance payments
- Elder care provider advisory charges
- Health care
- Medication and prescription drugs
- Eating out
- Entertainment
- Leisure/recreation/hobbies
- Travel/vacation
- Family gift-giving
- Donations
- Other spending (such as one-time purchase of various assets, major repairs, emergencies, etc.)

You will need to further break down some of these categories. Look at the chart that follows, which deals with costs for the various types of housing.

Housing costs: Basic	Housing costs: In-home care
Mortgage payments	Mortgage payments
Rent	Rent
Property taxes	Property taxes

Water & sewer	Water & sewer
Regular maintenance & upkeep	Regular maintenance & upkeep
Home insurance	Home insurance
Monthly condominium fees	Monthly condominium fees
	Homemaker
	Meal delivery
	Less: insurance coverage or other subsidies

Housing costs: Assisted-living facility	Housing costs: Long-term care facility
Rent	All-inclusive LTC facility charges
Meal preparation	Other facility charges
Other facility charges	Less: insurance coverage or other subsidies
Less: insurance coverage or other subsidies	

Other spending categories also have subcategories:

Utilities	Transportation
Heating	Public transportation (buses and taxis)
Electricity	Gasoline and fuel
Gas	Vehicle maintenance and repairs
Telephone	Vehicle insurance
Cellular phone	Parking charges
Cablevision	
Internet	

Insurance
Life and accidental death insurance
Extended health insurance
Dental insurance
Travel insurance
Critical illness insurance
Long-term care insurance

When creating your budget, you must carefully consider all elements of an expense.

You biggest costs will most likely be housing and utilities. If at all possible, on retirement you should eliminate your mortgage or at least drastically reduce the balance. Consider downsizing your home or relocating to a smaller community with a lower cost of living. See Chapter 9 for more ideas on housing choices.

At some point, however, you may need to move to an assisted-living or long-term care facility. At this time, approximately 9 million American retirees require long-term care. Apart from some limited exceptions, Medicare does not cover this expense. It also holds true for Canadian retirees that only medically necessary long-term care is covered by the country's universal health care plan.

In-home care, assisted living, or long-term care can take a big bite out of your savings. As a hedge against this expense, think about buying long-term care insurance (discussed below). Keep in mind, however, that for most retirees, the average length of stay in long-term care is no more than five years. Take care not to over-insure and pay premiums on benefits that you may not fully use. (For more information on long-term care, see Chapter 9 on housing choices.)

Insurance

Careful review of your existing insurance policies will help you with your retirement planning. Your insurance needs will change upon retirement, and your coverage needs may change, too. Ask yourself the following questions:

- Do I have adequate insurance?
- Do I have the right types of insurance?
- Am I over-insured?

These questions may best be answered by consulting with a fee-based (as opposed to a commission-based) certified financial planner and an insurance broker. It will be money well spent, and you'll know the advice you received is truly objective and has your best interests in mind.

Today's insurance market offers many new and innovative products, including —

- life insurance,
- disability insurance,
- extended health insurance,
- dental care insurance,
- critical illness insurance, and
- long-term care insurance.

When it comes to life and health-related insurance, the sooner you start a policy, the more attractive the price. Don't delay. The longer you wait, the more prohibitive the cost. Worse yet, you may risk being uninsurable due to an unexpected diagnosis of a terminal illness or its symptoms!

Think about whether or not it would be useful for you to have the various types of insurance discussed here.

Life insurance

There are many reasons for having life insurance on retirement. You can use life insurance as a means to leave something for your loved ones or favorite charities, leave a legacy, and as a means to pay your taxes on death. If your estate has outstanding debts, the benefit payout on your death can be used to settle them — which means your executor will not be forced to sell your estate's assets just to cover your debts.

Disability insurance

You will probably not need disability insurance after you retire, as such coverage is meant to provide benefits to workers who are unable to work due to an accident or illness. You may want to retain partial coverage if you continue working part-time on retirement, especially if you need the extra income to supplement your retirement lifestyle.

Critical illness insurance

Critical illness insurance, however, could be very useful to you. A typical policy usually provides the insured with a sum of money when a certain illness or health condition (specified under the policy) occurs. This sum of money is for you to spend as you see fit, and comes with no restrictions. The payments are designed to help you cover additional medical treatments or special medications, or even an extended trip if your illness is diagnosed as terminal. As with other kinds of health insurance, the earlier you sign up for the policy, the smaller the premium.

Long-term care insurance

Due to increased longevity, aging boomers and their parents are more apt to consider long-term care (LTC) insurance. There's a real likelihood they will need major home care for at least some of their passive retirement years, and they will possibly also (as mentioned above) move into an assisted-living or full-care facility at some point — and that's expensive. Private care facilities can cost thousands of dollars a month.

To protect your assets, consider purchasing LTC insurance to help you defray this cost. To determine how much coverage you'll need to purchase, first try to determine what your actual costs for long-term care might be. There may be some subsidies or government support for this type of care available to you in your jurisdiction. A good place to start your search for possible subsidies is the Administration on Aging (AOA) website in the US or your provincial ministry of health in Canada. Shop around and investigate the types of facilities in your area, determine the level and quality of care each can give, get answers on the costs for each facility, and think carefully about how much you can afford to pay. Armed with this information, you'll find it easier to decide how much LTC insurance you need to take out to help you fund your care in your passive retirement years.

Keep in mind, also, that not all retirees need LTC insurance. In addition, watch out to make sure you are not buying coverage that you may not use. Many retirees do not need long-term care. They have sufficient family help on a daily basis. Others are healthy and active, and stay relatively independent well into their nineties.

There are also many retirees who have accumulated adequate asset bases over their working lifetime to have sufficient resources to fund their own LTC needs. They would liquidate some of their investments and assets when the time comes to pay for the needed LTC costs.

For those who are considering LTC insurance, note that there are many different types of policies and coverage available. It is crucial to do your homework ahead of time. Make certain that before buying any policy, you have the answers to these questions:

- Which services are covered? Are nursing homes, assisted living, home care, and/or other types of care covered?
- How much does the policy cover, in dollars-per-day terms?
- Is a hospital visit required to trigger benefits?
- Is the coverage scaled to inflation so that purchasing power will always remain constant, no matter when the benefit is paid?

- Are pre-existing conditions covered without a waiting period?
- Are Alzheimer's and other mental disorders covered?

Answers to these and other questions are important to your understanding of what you are buying in a LTC policy. Help from a certified financial planner specializing in retirement planning will steer you in the right direction.

Check the American Association of Retired Persons' (AARP) website for useful links and other information on LTC insurance. See the Resources section for contact information.

Health insurance

Health care insurance is also important.

Canadian retirees will find themselves in the fortunate situation of having most medically necessary services covered by affordable universal health care. Prescription drug costs may also be covered, but the amount of this coverage is income-dependent and varies by province. Canadian readers who want to broaden their coverage beyond what is provided through the government program can purchase extended health care and dental insurance. These policies generally pay, partially or in full, for prescription drugs, various therapies, and basic eye and dental care needs.

The reality in the US is different. America is one of the few developed nations without universal health care coverage. But the good news is that retirees aged 65 and over are covered by Medicare.

Medicare is a federal health insurance program available to people in that age group. The health insurance is available in two parts: Medicare Part A, which is hospital insurance; and Medicare Part B, which is medical insurance. To learn more about the specific coverage available to you, check the Medicare website or contact your regional office. See the Resources section for contact information.

Medicare drug-discount cards can often save you 10 percent to 25 percent of the cost of prescription drugs, depending on the kind of drug you need. There are many different cards for many different drugs, so before enrolling, find out which card is appropriate for your health situation. You can only get one Medicare-endorsed drug-discount card. These cards are available until 2006, when Medicare's prescription-drug benefit will take effect and these cards will no longer be necessary.

If you plan on retiring before age 65, you must find your own health insurance coverage. You do not want to be without health insurance. Without it, a serious illness could mean financial catastrophe for you. It could wipe out your life's savings and completely derail your retirement plan.

Find out if your present employer provides benefits to retirees. If your employer does not provide retiree health benefits, you may need to look to private insurance, even if it is costly. Depending on the condition of your health, your financial situation, and the jurisdiction in which you plan to retire, the cost varies greatly. Understand, though, that it will likely be expensive.

There are some options that can help to bring down the cost of health premiums, thereby allowing you to bridge your coverage if you are hoping to take an early retirement. Consider the following options:

- *Catastrophic insurance:* This kind of insurance can make health insurance affordable. The policy is designed to cover health care costs beyond a certain amount. It comes with a large deductible, usually $5,000 or more.

- *Short-term insurance:* Short-term insurance can fill the gap if you are only a short time away from turning 65 and qualifying for Medicare.

- *Group insurance through an association:* This option may offer premium relief to group members, making it more affordable.

- *COBRA* (Consolidated Omnibus Budget Reconciliation Act): A federal law allowing you to continue your employer-provided health care coverage for another 18 months after you retire. You must apply within 60 days of leaving your job. Depending on the state, COBRA can be expensive. Nonetheless, it can be an attractive option for early retirees with pre-existing health conditions.

The bottom line on health care insurance: it is complicated and expensive. Different states have different laws. You must do your homework on this subject before taking early retirement. Be prepared to work until age 65 if you are unable to obtain affordable health care insurance before Medicare kicks in, or be very prepared to gamble on not having any serious illness before age 65.

Once you reach 65 and qualify for Medicare, you may want to supplement your coverage by purchasing Medigap or another private supplemental insurance. Depending on the plan, they may cover costs such as Medicare deductibles, routine eye exams, hearing aids, and even dental care. Check the AARP website for more information on the various supplemental medicare plans sold by private insurance companies.

Your Budget and Your Choices

Planning for retirement spending takes some thought. It's to your advantage to take a broad view. What follows are some important considerations that will directly affect your retirement plan:

1. Community

   The size of your community as well as its location and proximity to your loved ones will affect your spending pattern. For example, if you plan on moving to a smaller, more remote community, you'll probably want a heavy-duty vehicle, in good running condition.

2. Lifestyle choices

   What are you planning to do for the rest of your life? Will you be traveling? If so, how, where, and how often? What hobbies and leisure activities are you going to pursue?

3. Activities

   In retirement, you need to develop activities that will take the place of work. Have you considered volunteer work? Will you start a home-based business? What about going back to school to get that law degree you always wanted?

4. Quality-of-life choices

   Don't forget to consider the lifestyle to which you are accustomed or to which you may look forward to experiencing. For ease of planning, when you consider your lifestyle, think about its "must haves" (those things you can't do without), its "like to haves" (those things that are pleasant and enjoyable, but not necessary), and those things to which you are indifferent and with which you may dispense.

5. Income level

   Will your pension and other income allow you to maintain the lifestyle of your choosing?

6. Types of insurance

   Examine your policies and incorporate the extent of their coverage into your plan.

7. Your health

   This factor will determine the extent of care (and its costs) for which you will need to plan.

8. Availability of assistance

   Your proximity to your loved ones and their willingness to assist you in your care can have an effect on your expenses.

9. Professional help

   Think about your level of knowledge on financial matters and the extent of professional help required. Will you need to hire advisers?

10. Communication with your partner and loved ones

    This matter is crucial. Making decisions together and making them known is good for your financial future!

11. Major and difficult life issues

    Consider all life-changing issues, such as end-of-life considerations, potential guardianship issues, and early gradual distribution of estate assets, then discuss these with your spouse or partner and make space for them in your plan.

Giving some thought to these considerations now can help you make your retirement budget more realistic, and therefore more workable. Take a look at the example below to see how lifestyle choices can affect a budget.

Bert and Joanne are healthy and active sixty-year-olds. They live about two hours away from their two grown children, in a small, semi-rural community. They would like to live no more than half an hour by car from their grown children, both of whom reside in the same big city on the West Coast. This "must have" decision means Bert and Joanne must relocate closer to an urban center, at an additional 20 percent more in housing costs and 15 percent more in food and sundries. But this decision also results in them saving 50 percent in transportation costs, as they can afford to give up one of their two vehicles. There are intangible benefits for them, too, in this situation: being closer to a large center, they are offered more community activities at affordable prices. They will have the pleasure of visiting their grandchildren on a more frequent basis.

Think about your own situation. If you have the travel bug, consider downsizing your home, possibly to a small studio condominium or mobile home. You may want to invest in an RV for touring the continent, or you may choose to fly or cruise to your destinations instead. The decision you make on your mode of travel will determine the amount of money you need to set aside to accommodate this choice, affecting both your housing and travel budgets.

If your health requires constant professional care, you will have to take this condition into account when choosing where to retire. You may need to be close to your doctors and other health specialists. You may want to be near a good hospital. You may even need to consider areas where there are reputable long-term care facilities, at a price you can afford. Do your homework, set your goals, and make your decisions. Plan your lifestyle ahead of time. Know which major changes you may be required to make.

Do you have expensive tastes, or are you thrifty? You need to understand this aspect of your personality, as it affects your budget greatly. If you have $200 a month for dining out, would you prefer to dine out once at a nice restaurant or four times at the neighborhood eatery? Or would you reduce the amount to $100 and save the rest for gifts for the grandchildren? Whatever the case, you must be realistic. You want to retire within your means.

You have choices. You just need to know what they are and decide in favor of the ones that are suitable for your circumstances.

Budgeting Downward

The perceived problem of budgeting your spending downward on retirement is not as onerous as it might seem. Luckily, most retirees find they can live on less when retired than they did while working. In fact, most retirees live on 70 percent or less of their annual preretirement income. Bear in mind, though, that the lower your working years' income was, the more this percentage will rise. Nonetheless, despite what you may have read or heard, most people do not need a large company pension and a million dollars in savings to live comfortably in retirement.

Why? Just look at the following:

- Most retirees have paid off their homes and are mortgage-free.

- Retirees' employment-related expenses (such as office wardrobes, transportation, and meals) are eliminated or drastically reduced.

- Income and social security taxes are lower for retirees or are eliminated altogether.

- Most retirees are no longer setting aside money for retirement and for their children's educations.

- The human "need to spend" tendency decreases with age.

- There are many opportunities for seniors' discounts. Just ask!

- There are many opportunities for seniors' freebies. Keep your eyes and ears open!

Even with all the advantages listed above, it is still imperative that you guard against eroding your asset base for your day-to-day living expenses, especially in your active retirement years. After all, you expect to be living for quite a few more years. You want to maintain or continue growing your assets until your passive retirement years, when you'll need those resources to cover extra help and medical costs. Depending on your circumstances, you may even want to consider turning your non-income producing assets into income-producing assets.

Set down your plan on paper. The Yearly Spending Budget Worksheets you will find online at <www.self-counsel.com .updates/after55/bonus.htm> can help you do this. There is one for each phase of retirement (Worksheet 6 for active retirees, Worksheet 7 for semi-active retirees, and Worksheet 8 for passive retirees). You will transfer to this sheet the figure for your total after-tax cash inflow from the Cash Inflow Worksheet you completed in Chapter 5. Once you've done that, proceed line by line through all the expense categories listed in the left-hand column, estimating both their per month and per year amounts. Any known expenses unique to you that are not listed on the form may be added on the blank lines after Extraordinary items. When you've completed this step, total all your expenses, and enter both the monthly and yearly total on the second to last line in the appropriate column. Then subtract your total expenses from your total after-tax cash inflow, and you'll see whether your budget will work as estimated or if you will have a shortfall.

Estimate the budget for the current lifestyle phase you are leading. Are you able to support yourself through it? You need to know what resources are available to you and whether or not they can meet your spending needs.

If you are in the active or semi-active retirement phase, you should also complete the yearly spending budget for your passive retirement years. Project the costs as if you are living it now, just so you have a rough estimate in today's dollars.

Keep in mind that when planning both your active and semi-active retirement spending budgets, your goal is to live within your means without touching your asset base. If, after preparing your budgets, you see there is a shortfall for the year, you must reconsider your lifestyle choices for active retirement. You must either lower your spending, or find a way to increase the income portion of your cash inflow so that your spending and your cash inflow are as equal as possible. You do not want to deplete your net worth base prematurely.

There are ways you can compensate for a shortfall. Options to increase cash inflow (such as working part time, delaying retirement, and starting a small business on the side) have already been discussed in a previous chapter. But you can also carefully adjust your spending downward to meet the resources you have on hand. Look at each spending category to determine if it can be reduced. For example, maybe that gym membership or the fancy cellular or cable package should go. Even foregoing a planned vacation is worth it if it can put you back on track.

Take a close look at Sample 6, which is the Yearly Spending Budget for Active Retirees for Bob and Jane. Observe the following:

- Their after-tax cash inflow as calculated (from Sample 4 in Chapter 5) is $44,900.

- Their estimated housing cost is minimal, as their home is mortgage free.

- Monthly cleaning services and summer yard maintenance are budgeted under In-home care and Yard maintenance.

- They budget minimal health care costs as they are both in good health and lead healthy lifestyles.

- Their insurance costs include life insurance as well as critical illness and health care insurance. They're fortunate to pay the preferred rate of $200 a month for this employer-sponsored health care plan.

- Their travel budget is their biggest expense item in their active retirement years at $8,400.

- They even have a reserve of $3,540 remaining for their discretionary spending for the year.

For Bob and Jane, their total after-tax cash inflow is sufficient for their current active retirement lifestyle. They are living within their means, even without receiving social security pensions or withdrawing from their qualified retirement accounts.

With the excess cash they have available, they may purchase some long-term care insurance to hedge their assistive care costs in their later retirement years.

For now, they are enjoying their travel, families, and friends. Their retirement living is full; planning has given them

Sample 6
YEARLY SPENDING BUDGET
(For active retirees)

Yearly Spending Budget Worksheet — Active Retirees
For the year ___2005___
For: ___Bob & Jane___

	Per Month	Yearly Total
(from Cash Inflow Worksheet)		
Total after tax cash inflow		**44,900**
Expenses		
Housing costs – basic	300	3,600
In-home care – house cleaning	50	600
Utilities	200	2,400
Yard maintenance	30	360
Food and sundries	600	7,200
Personal grooming	100	1,200
Medical and dental costs	100	1,200
Prescription drugs & medication	100	1,200
Pet care and supplies		
Insurance (all)	400	4,800
Eating out and entertainment	200	2,400
Leisure & recreation	200	2,400
Church & religious contributions		
Local transportation		
Vehicle costs	300	3,600
Travel	700	8,400
Extraordinary items:		
home renovations & major repairs		1,000
furnishings		1,000
reserve/allowance — for discretionary spending!		3,540
Total expenses		**44,900**
Net cash surplus (shortfall)		**$0**

the knowledge and security that they will be financially sound for the many years to come.

Note that Bob and Jane also completed the Yearly Spending Budget Worksheet for Passive Retirees (see Sample 7). They wish to know now if they have sufficient resources to support their passive retirement lifestyle years if one of them has to move to a nursing home and the other requires additional in-home care.

Based on their projected cash inflow (see Sample 5 in Chapter 5) and spending budget, they appear to be in good shape. They know they need to be flexible and will review their plans yearly. When it becomes necessary, they will rethink and revise their plans to make certain they continue to live within their means.

Sample 7
YEARLY SPENDING BUDGET
(For passive retirees)

Yearly Spending Budget Worksheet — Passive Retirees
For the year ___2005___
For: ___Bob & Jane___

	Per Month	Yearly Total
(from Cash Inflow Worksheet)		
Total after tax cash inflow		**81,000**
Expenses		
Housing costs – basic	300	3,600
In-home care – house cleaning	100	1,200
In-home care – meal preparation	150	1,800
In-home care – meal delivery		
In-home care – assistive living	600	7,200
Senior living – facility charges	3,200	38,400
Senior living – other charges		
Long term care – facility charges		
Long term care – other charges		
Less: care insurance coverage		
Less: care subsidies		
Utilities	200	2,400
Yard maintenance		
Food & sundries	200	2,400
Personal grooming	200	2,400
Medical and dental costs	500	6,000
Prescription drugs	500	6,000
Pet care and supplies		
Eldercare provider advisory charges	100	1,200

Sample 7 — Continued

Insurance (all)	400	4,800
Eating out and entertainment	100	1,200
Leisure and recreation	100	1,200
Local transportation	100	1,200
Vehicle costs		
Travel		
Extraordinary items:		
Total expenses		**81,000**
Net cash surplus (shortfall)		**$0**

Chapter 7
READING THE CRYSTAL BALL

All retirees need to have some idea of whether or not they have enough resources to live on comfortably for the rest of their lives. Your passive retirement years may seem a long way off, but you'll be making a savvy move by thinking ahead now. That is why it is wise to gaze into your crystal ball and see if you can project into your financial future, even if it's a bit hazy!

Aside from government and company pensions, you will likely look to your investments and qualified or registered retirement savings to provide the additional funds you'll need for passive retirement. Will they have grown enough to support those extra costs when you need to consider assisted living or long-term care? By looking into the crystal ball now, you can start planning to maximize your resources to take care of yourself and your spouse in your passive years. This chapter discusses ways to estimate your future resources and spending.

If you have even some rough estimated figures, you'll take comfort in the knowledge that you have some control over your resources, and it makes your long-term planning that much more easy and predictable. It will also give you a sense of security, control, and independence. Knowing you'll have enough money will give you some degree of choice, even when the time comes that you'll be needing assistance in your daily living.

Conversely, if your estimates show that you do not have sufficient resources to support your passive retirement lifestyle, you can change your situation today to improve on your future financial picture. You may need to delay retirement or cut short that annual vacation, but your future is totally under your control and you can make it work. It's all in the long-term planning.

Finally, you may want to plan on leaving something in your will for your loved ones and/or preferred charities. If you understand your full retirement picture, you've already begun your estate plan.

Here's How You Begin ...

Even if you are still some years away from your passive retirement, you should complete the Cash Inflow worksheet for Passive Retirees (see Chapter 5) and Yearly Spending Budget for Passive Retirees (see Chapter 6). You need to look ahead and estimate what cash sources are available to you and what your expenses will be when you reach passive retirement. You can start by estimating them as if you are living your passive retirement years today. For now, estimate both your cash sources and expenses in today's dollar.

Two of the major expenses in your passive retirement years will be assisted living and long-term care costs. You'll want to do some research to find out how much these would cost should you require them today. You'll need to honestly examine your own situation and decide whether or not you anticipate needing some assisted care or full-blown long-term care. One clue to help you with this estimate is your current health and healthy (or unhealthy) lifestyle choices. Another telltale clue is your family history. Look to your parents and grandparents' longevity and health history. Doing so will give you some idea as to how much care you will need in your passive retirement years.

Use the Yearly Spending Budget for Passive Retirees Worksheet to list and total up the likely expenses of your passive years. You can deduct it from the anticipated total cash inflow as calculated in your Cash Inflow Worksheet for Passive Retirees. If there is a surplus, you'll know your passive retirement years are likely to be financially adequate.

If you anticipate a shortfall, determine how much you need to continue to save and invest today to cushion this shortfall some years away. Again, revisit chapters 4 and 8 for ideas on how to compensate for the shortfall. Examine ways to —

- live below your means today in active or semi-active retirement so that you can save more and invest the difference;

- consider using your home to help finance your passive retirement needs (such as renting out part of your home or downsizing your home);

- use the Savings Chart Summary Guide to roughly estimate the growth of your extra investments before you reach your passive retirement years; and/or

- prolong your capacity to earn part-time employment or self-employment income while in active retirement.

Look at the following example:

Joan is in her active retirement years. She completed her Yearly Spending Budget for Passive Retirees and Cash Inflow Worksheet for Passive Retirees and anticipated a shortfall of $300 a month when she reaches retirement in 15 years. Looking ahead at her future situation, she figures that by downsizing her present home now, she will net $80,000 to invest. Using the Savings Chart Summary Guide in Chapter 4, with Joan expecting to earn a 4 percent return, after tax, on her investments, her $80,000 will grow to $144,080 in 15 years ($80,000 x factor 1.801). This estimated extra cushion, based only on a broad projection, will ease Joan's concerns about her passive retirement. Knowing that will also serve as a catalyst to make Joan act today so that she proceeds with her plan to downsize her home.

Ideally, over time, through the magic of compounding, your investments and registered savings will grow enough to cover any additional costs associated with your passive retirement. However, you may need professional advice now to determine how best to grow your savings. Depending on your circumstances, planning matters for you to bear in mind include the following:

- Where reinvestments should occur, either inside or outside your qualified or registered retirement accounts
- Which spouse's accounts you should withdraw from and how much (for tax purposes)
- If and when you should apply for early government pensions
- Tax rules and planning considerations
- Estate-planning considerations

If you have a business, selling the business to fund your assistive care should be part of your plan. Of course, selling your home, if you haven't already done so, is also a way to raise funds.

The Savings Chart Summary Guide in Chapter 4 will show you how much your pretax savings can grow to by the time you may need to tap into them for the extra costs of passive retirement. For example, if you've got $200,000 in your qualified or registered retirement savings today, the account would be worth $479,400 in 15 years if you expect an average return of 6 percent ($200,000 x factor 2.397).

However, that total will grow to $641,400 if you leave it invested for 20 years ($200,000 x factor 3.207), but to just $358,200 if you leave it alone for only 10 years ($200,000 x factor 1.791).

You can use the same chart to estimate your after-tax investment growth over time. For example, if you have $200,000 in an investment account today and your expected return is 5 percent, with a 20 percent tax rate for 15 years, your growth will be based on the 4 percent factor (5 percent less (20 percent of 5 percent)). That total will be $360,200 ($200,000 x factor 1.801). A more modest growth, but that's because taxes on the income have already been accounted for.

Please note the Savings Chart Summary Guide assumes a consistent return from year to year. It should be used as a guide for projection purposes only. Your actual return will probably be different.

The same 5 percent return on investment, on an after-tax (assuming 20 percent) basis of 4 percent, will grow to $438,200 if you have it invested for 20 years ($200,000 x factor 2.191), but only to $296,000 if you leave it invested for 10 years ($200,000 x factor 1.480).

If your after-tax rate of return does not work out to be a whole number, for simplicity's sake, round it up or down to the nearest whole number rate. For example, for a rate of return of 6 percent for 15 years, and a tax rate of 25 percent, the after-tax rate of return is 4.5 percent. Round this up to 5 percent and use the 5 percent factor to get your estimate. Again, keep in mind that these numbers are only estimates and do not need to be exact.

The examples above ignored graduated tax rates and restrictions and tax rules related to qualified or registered retirement accounts, such as required minimum withdrawal rates. You must build these restrictions into your own plan when estimating. Nonetheless, the chart is a means of helping you gauge the growth over time of your investment nest egg.

If you are unsure of how you'll completely fund assisted or long-term care needs in your passive retirement, or if you plan to preserve your estate for your beneficiaries, think about buying some long-term care insurance now. (For more information on long-term care insurance, see the insurance section in Chapter 6.)

The government does provide some assistance in medically necessary long-term care, but it is often quite restrictive. Usually, you will receive no financial help if you choose to stay in your own home and have in-home help. Also, if you demand a certain level of quality care, you may have to pay for it yourself. The insurance coverage for long-term care varies widely. Make sure you shop around and compare plans to find the right one for you and your spouse, and start making your plans for it today.

Depending on your and/or your spouse's health and family history, you'll want to estimate the costs for living your passive retirement years in comfort and security. You may want to factor in expenses for two different households, as only one of you may need to move to a care facility while the other remains at home.

For example, you may be well enough to stay on your own, but your spouse may require long-term care. You'll have to factor this extra cost into your future budget. Do you think you have enough income and savings to support two homes? What does the kind of long-term care you want cost? What types are available in your community? What subsidies are available, and how do you apply for them? These and other questions are best answered ahead of time. Do your research. Various checklists are included online at <www.self-counsel .com/updates/after55/bonus.htm> to check and compare care facilities in your desired communities, in advance. By planning now, you are giving yourself time to consider other means of funding your care.

There are other options, too. One unpopular — but logical — option is for you to work full-time for a few extra years to give your retirement accounts more time to accumulate and grow. Another is to cut back on your spending in your active retirement years to save for your passive retirement years.

Take a look at Sample 5 (in Chapter 5), Bob and Jane's Cash Inflow for Passive Retirement, and Sample 7 (in Chapter 6), their Yearly Spending Budget for Passive Retirees. As mentioned previously, they are currently both 56, healthy, and active.

They are looking into the (they hope, very distant) future, when they may require assistive care in their daily living. They want to know if (were those years happening today and were they themselves much older) they'd be able to provide for themselves. They have used the Cash Inflow Worksheet for Passive Retirees and the Yearly Spending Budget Worksheet for Passive Retirees to help estimate this scenario in today's dollar.

Observe the following:

- Their expected cash inflow, after tax, is increased to $81,000. This is due to the addition of government pensions and qualified or registered retirement account withdrawals. They have also allowed for increased investment income over time and some dispositions of mutual-fund investments.

- They will not be working part-time, and so have eliminated income from this source.

- They estimate that one of them will require long-term care in a nursing home, while the other remains at home with in-home care. Based on their research in their community, in-home and facility-care costs make up the majority of their budget.

- They will have no vehicle expenses and little or no travel costs.

- Along with other estimated expenses, their budget is projected to equal $81,000, which equals the amount they estimate as their after-tax cash inflow.

They can see on paper that their finances in their future passive retirement years will be in good shape. They know there is enough cash inflow to support their needs at that stage in their lives. Other options to consider now include the following:

- Should they consider long-term care insurance today to cushion the cost of assistive care in the future?

- What supplementary health care plan is suitable for their needs?

- What (if any) legacy or estate do they wish to leave behind?

Peeking into the crystal ball can offer you insights into your future needs so you can plan properly for them now. Be aware, however, that unpredictable events can derail the best-laid retirement plans, and can do so at the most unexpected times. There are things that you simply can't plan for in advance, as the list below illustrates:

- *Unpredictable rates of return on your investments:* Markets and their underlying economies are unpredictable. Think 9/11, the tragic event that caused the global market to plummet overnight.

- *Unpredictable future tax-rule changes:* You can never predict with certainty what changes future governments will make to the present income tax system, just as you cannot predict how income tax rates will look ten years (even two years) from today.

- *Unpredictable pension reform:* Governments and corporations are well aware of the potential liability aging baby boomers represent to treasuries and coffers. Legislative changes may be in the works in the near future to minimize the negative impact of graying North Americans on public coffers and corporate bottom lines.

- *Unpredictable health, medical, and lifestyle discoveries and changes:* The pace of new discoveries in technologies and biotechnologies is mind-boggling. More breakthroughs will continue to enable baby boomers to live not only longer but also better lives. Only time will tell how these discoveries will affect the lifestyle of the baby boomers of the future.

When you gaze into your distant future, you must remember to stay flexible. Commit yourself to yearly reviews. Never stop looking into that crystal ball, and adjust your plan accordingly.

Chapter 8

USING YOUR HOME TO FINANCE YOUR RETIREMENT

If you're like most retirees, your home is probably your most valuable asset. You've heard the saying, "House rich, cash poor." This maxim often applies to retirees whose equity is tied up in their homes. Their income-generating investments and retirement-saving assets are minimal — and the result is that they have minimal income from investments, which diminishes their overall quality of life.

Ideally, you need to build up not only your home equity, but also your retirement savings as well as other income-producing investments for a well-balanced asset base. But what if your home is where you have most of your money? This chapter discusses some options for you to consider.

An obvious choice is renting out part of your home for income (this option was briefly discussed in Chapter 5). But there are other ideas that may suit you better. They involve financing your retirement using your home, and are as follows:

1. Downsize your home, and invest the excess cash from the sale.

2. Sell outright and invest the cash.

3. Use a reverse mortgage.

4. Borrow against your home equity, and invest the money.

Downsizing Your Home

You may be very attached to the home you have now, but if you find yourself without sufficient income for your retirement, you must ask yourself some tough questions. Do you really need the four-bedroom, three-bathroom house with the huge backyard? Your three grown children and their families may visit, but they are unlikely to stay for long periods of time or all at the same time. An obvious solution to the problem of having too much house is to downsize your home. You may find that a two-bedroom bungalow is more suitable for you now, or even a condominium might be an option, to avoid yard work and reduce upkeep and maintenance costs.

Often, retirees can relocate to a smaller home and still stay in the same neighborhood. Doing so enables them to free up some needed cash for living and investments, and at the same time helps them reduce their maintenance and upkeep expenses. A hidden benefit of exercising this option is that they end up with less housework!

You may profit even more by selling your home and moving to a town with a lower cost of living. You must, however, weigh that option very carefully, as there may be drawbacks that come along with that choice. For example, you might find that you spend more on transportation to visit with relatives and friends.

Don't overlook the possible tax implications of your decision. In the US, when you sell your home, you may face having to pay capital gains tax on the sale. Fortunately for Canadians, there is no capital gains tax on the sale of your home if it is your principal residence. You would be very wise to seek professional advice in this area of finance before you make this move. Consult a certified financial planner or a professional accountant before you move ahead.

To see if downsizing would work for you, use the Home Downsizing Comparison Worksheet (Worksheet 9) available online at <www.self-counsel.com/updates/after55/bonus.htm>. This is a worthwhile exercise, as it helps you determine whether downsizing is worth your while. Write down in the middle column of the worksheet the amounts for all the expenses you incur to run your existing home. Then, in the right-hand column, enter estimates of the amounts of all the expenses you think you would incur if you downsized to a smaller house. On completion, Part 1 of the worksheet will show you what you will save monthly in overhead and other costs by making the change.

Part 2 helps you calculate how much extra before-tax income can be generated yearly from investing the excess cash received on the sale of your home. Armed with this information, your decision should now be clearer to you.

Sell and Rent

It may be worth your while to sell your home, and instead of purchasing a smaller one, simply rent. The idea of not owning your own space may be unappealing to you, but if your plans for the future do not include spending a lot of time at home, this option may be the most practical for you.

For example, it makes sense to sell your house if you are planning to travel for a few years. You may wish to rent a small pied-à-terre in town if you plan on returning often or if you just wish to maintain a home base, no matter how small.

This option is best, too, if you know that you'll need a serious assisted-living arrangement soon and are on a waiting list to get into your preferred facility or retirement home. Selling your house now may also be advantageous to you because of the favorable market conditions.

The cash from the sale of your home can be invested to fund your rent and other retirement expenses. If you have any excess income after your expenses are covered, you can reinvest it for continued growth.

Be aware that selling your home may result in insufficient investment return to cover your rent. You must do your due diligence, think through carefully whether this is the right move for you given your investment knowledge, risk-tolerance level, and personal circumstances.

Reverse Mortgage (US)

Don't have quite enough to retire on yet? Then look closer to home — literally at your home! A concept started in France 100 years ago, the reverse mortgage is now widely used in the US, and has been for more than 25 years. If you are not able or willing to move, if you do not want to sell your home but you need cash, a reverse mortgage may be the solution for you.

You may qualify for a reverse mortgage if you are 62 years of age or older and own your own home. The most attractive feature of a reverse mortgage is that it allows you to supplement your income, tax free.

Residential properties have increased in value over the last few years. A reverse mortgage lets you tap into the equity you have right under your roof. It is designed especially for seniors who may have a lot of their equity tied up in their homes and wish to access it without selling.

In exchange for the money you receive from a reverse mortgage, you give up part of the equity built up in your home. You also pay a rate of interest for the money advanced to you. Repayment of the money is deferred until you sell, die, or permanently move from your home. If you are married, repayment is postponed until both you and your spouse die.

You can choose to receive a lump sum amount, monthly cash payments, or a combination of both. Check with your local state's US Housing and Urban Development (HUD) office to obtain a list of HUD-approved reverse mortgage lenders. You should also meet with a local HUD housing counselor before entering into a reverse mortgage. There is little or no cost for this service. See the Resources section at the back of this book and your local telephone directory for contact information on HUD.

The American Association of Retired Persons (AARP) is another good source of information on reverse mortgages. See the Resources section for contact information.

Keep in mind that reverse mortgages are not for everyone. You are giving up sole ownership of your home and using up equity you have accumulated. There may be little or nothing left in your family home for your children and grandchildren. Be aware of the potential drain on your estate by using a reverse mortgage as your source of cash for living.

Reverse Mortgage (Canada)

Similar to the US program, the Canadian reverse mortgage has been around for almost 20 years. Its terms are very similar to the American version. According to Statistics Canada, the biggest asset of a Canadian family unit is its principal residence, accounting, on average, for more than 37 percent of the family's total assets. Therefore, Canadians have more than a third of everything they own invested in their homes. It's only natural to think about the possibility of converting your home from a simple asset to a cash-generating asset.

It's normal to have your assets make money for you and finance your retirement. You should not overlook using your home in this way. Depending on your situation, you may want to take out a reverse mortgage to —

- supplement your monthly retirement income,
- pay off some major debts, and/or
- delay withdrawing taxable retirement income.

For more information, contact the Canadian Home Income Plan (CHIP). Check the Resources section for contact information.

Home Equity Line of Credit (HELOC)

Readers will be interested to know that it has become increasingly popular for homeowners to use home-equity lines of credit to make major purchases, invest in the stock markets, and consolidate debts.

These loans are desirable because they are flexible. On approval, you are usually given permission to draw on an amount of money, up to a predetermined maximum, for whatever purpose you wish. At any time, you can take out as much or as little below the maximum as you choose. Interest is chargeable from the time the money is withdrawn and is payable monthly. Depending on your credit worthiness, the rate of interest is usually very attractive, and far below the going consumer debt rate. You can repay all or part of the loan at any time, with no penalty. The minimum payment per month is usually the interest amount. Generally speaking (in the US only), the interest is tax deductible on the first $100,000 of HELOC for most borrowers. In Canada, the interest is tax deductible only if the loan is used for investment and business purposes.

The line of credit uses your home as collateral. You can take the opportunity to turn part of your home into income-producing assets by using the money from the loan to buy investments for income and growth.

Keep in mind a home-equity line of credit has serious drawbacks:

- A home-equity line of credit is a mortgage (or a second mortgage) on your home that includes a "balance owing may be called by the bank at any time" on-demand clause. Should you fail to repay your loan amount owing on demand, you could be facing a home foreclosure.

- Depending on your investment choices, you can literally gamble your home away if you decide to choose high-risk investments.

- There is a risk of your investments failing while you still owe the same amount as borrowed from the line of credit. The worst-case scenario can be that you find yourself with investments of no value and your loan for them still fully unpaid.

- The fees for setting up the line of credit are similar to setting up a mortgage and can be expensive. You need to shop around.

- Most home-equity lines of credit are variable rate based. When interest rate rises, your cost of borrowing will go up.

- You may be tempted to use the line of credit to pay for other expenses rather than investing, creating a debt-ridden nightmare for yourself if you let it get out of control.

Although a home-equity line of credit represents an opportunity to use part of your home for investment purposes, it is considered a risky move. Be aware of the pitfalls of this choice before moving ahead with it. However, if it works as planned, you will achieve greater income for your retirement, better investment-portfolio diversification, and continued growth of your assets.

Chapter 9
HOUSING CHOICES

Your housing needs may change when you retire. According to statistics, most people, by the time they're ready to stop working, have homes that are mortgage free or very close to it. You may choose to move from your current home to something different. You may sell your house and buy a condo instead, move to a smaller town for a total change of environment, or decide to be footloose and move into your RV.

Another reality is that as you grow older, your overall needs may change. Your need for care by others may increase. Planning for these changes will allow you to assess your options calmly and objectively, well ahead of the time you'll be required to make your move.

Housing will be one of your biggest expenses on retirement, and, if you don't pay close attention to it, it can drain your resources very quickly. You'll find it's well worth the effort to plan for the cost of your changing housing needs, and to allow for adjustments over time as you move from active to semi-active, to passive retirement.

Each of these stages comes with different housing needs, and each may require a different housing option. For your active retirement, you may want to assess your housing needs based on your activities. Are you looking forward to a great deal of traveling or will you be pursuing hobbies or interests closer to home? Think carefully about your plans, as these decisions will affect your housing requirements.

If your plans involve making a number of extended trips for vacations each year, you may want to downsize your home. However, if you want to start a home-based business or pursue an interest from home, you may need to stay put and even renovate your current home to accommodate your new venture.

Regardless of the type of home you choose for this stage of your retirement, remember that housing costs for an active retiree should exceed no more than 30 percent of the total household budget. For example, if your annual retirement budget is $45,000, your housing costs should ideally be $13,500 or less (or $1,125 per month). This amount can be reduced if you plan to supplement your travel budget, or it can be a bit more if you are to use your home for a part-time business or income-generating hobby.

As you move into semi-active retirement, your housing needs may change. You have now traded your RV for a one-level condominium or mobile home. You may wish to engage non-professional assistance for housekeeping, yard work, and meal preparation. You may find at this stage of your retirement that your housing costs may go down as you move into smaller quarters, but your home-care costs are starting to rise.

When you reach your passive-retirement years, you may be fully dependent on other people for daily living and care. Your housing costs may be the all-inclusive long-term care facility charges, which basically include most of your daily living expenses. While this option may seem dramatically expensive, you can also expect to scale back just as dramatically on other things such as travel, housing overheads, and groceries.

What follows here are some options for you to consider, taking into account your changing needs for each stage of your retirement.

Housing Options for Active Retirees

The first two options discussed in this section are best suited to younger and healthy retirees. For these options to work for you, you should be active, independent, and require no assistance in your daily living.

Option 1: Same house? Different house? Too much house?

If you find yourself caught between wanting to stay in your current home but not being sure it's right for you at this time of your life, you need to examine your situation carefully. Here are some questions to help you clarify whether you should keep your home or move to a different arrangement. Be aware that there are no right or wrong answers; these questions are designed to help you see the big picture of your housing situation as it exists now:

- How often are you away from home?

  _____ months/year

- How often do you entertain out-of-town visitors at home?

  _____ times/year

- How many rooms in the house are vacant at least 70 percent of the time?

  _____

- Are there too many stairs in the current home?

  _____

- Do you feel safe at all times in your current home?

  _____

- Do you like your present neighborhood and current neighbors?

  _____

- Would you prefer to be in a retirement community?

  _____

- Would you be more comfortable in a condominium, where there is round-the-clock security?

  _____

- Do you garden? Would you mind giving up gardening?

  _____

- Would you be happy in a mobile home?

  _____

- Would you be happy relocating to another neighborhood or town?

  _____

- If you want to stay where you are now, does your home require ongoing home repairs and maintenance?

  _____

- Are you handy around your home?

  _____

- Are major renovations required to bring your current home up to acceptable comfort and safety standards?

  _____

- If yes, what is the estimated cost of these renovations? $_____

- Can you afford the necessary renovations and upgrades?

  _____

If you decide that now is the time for you to make a move from your current home, there are a number of housing arrangements you can consider:

- *Independent living:* If your present home no longer suits you, you could move to a smaller family home or condo in the same community, a neighboring community, across town, across the country, or to another country, if you wish.

- *Active retirement communities:* These range from low- to high-end communities that are geared to attracting younger, mobile, and active retirees. They usually come complete with a given retirement lifestyle. Types of housing include —
  - mobile homes,
  - manufactured homes,
  - condominiums,
  - townhouses, and/or
  - single-family homes (ideally all on one level).

- *Home sharing:* There are different ways to home share. Two retirees or couples may pool resources to co-own a home, or one owns and the other rents, or one owns and the other works for his or her rent. There are benefits to home sharing. Not only will your overall housing costs decrease, but you may also gain new friendships and an extra degree of security around your home.

- *Recreational vehicle (RV)* or houseboat living: If you have wanderlust and wish to travel but want to do it in home-style comfort, RVing or houseboating may be for you. What better way to see the world: you go at your own pace, you don't have to pack and unpack, and your fridge is always within five feet of you!

  Part-time RVing in your own or another country allows you a great deal of flexibility. There are clubs that provide their members with a wealth of RV-related resources, including ratings on RV parks and campgrounds across North America and Mexico.

If you plan to RV in another country, be certain you have obtained all the appropriate and necessary paperwork, including insurance coverage, and be aware that you may require professional assistance to obtain the required documentation if it is written in another language. (For example, the main language of Mexico is Spanish; the main language in the province of Quebec, Canada, is French.)

The houseboating option comes with less mobility, as these communities are usually limited to small lakes and rivers. You would probably be renting your houseboat rather than owning one.

(Check the RV and travel contacts in the Resources section.)

- *Foreign home:* This option can be ideal for retirees who are completely free of ties to their home country. Housing abroad can be extremely affordable. However, be aware also of the drawbacks. Remember to consider —

  - the political stability of the chosen country,
  - the quality of health care,
  - the crime rate,
  - the overall quality of life, and
  - the overall tax implications of living abroad or emigrating.

  It's not an option to be taken lightly. Do your homework, and obtain professional legal and tax advice before you make your move.

As you can see from the many choices available, active retirees really need to think through their active retirement goals before making any housing change. Don't rush. Take your time, and talk to your spouse if you are part of a couple, to ensure your choice is the right one for the duration of your active retirement years. Who knows — you may even find that staying put is the right decision for you for now.

Option 2: Moving in with your grown child and his or her family

This option is also suited to passive retirees; however, if you've become single again and prefer not to live alone, this choice may be viable for you. But before agreeing to move in with your grown child and his or her family, you may need to give serious thought to the following questions:

- Will the new arrangement affect your current good relationship with your offspring?
- Are you used to your independence? In what ways would it be restricted by such a move?
- What are your grown child's expectations of this new arrangement?
- Will you be expected to help with caring for your grandchild(ren)?
- Will you be happy with them? Will they be happy with you?
- Are you emotionally suited to living in close proximity to your children?
- Does your culture normally find this arrangement acceptable?
- How many physical modifications will be needed to upgrade the existing living space to accommodate the new arrangement?
- Specifically, how much will it cost to renovate?
- Who will pay for these renovations and upgrades? (There are extra grab bars, non-skid tiles for the bathroom, and maybe a safety railing for the backstairs to consider.)
- How will daily living expenses be shared?

This option comes with several variations, including —

- a self-contained apartment on your child's property,
- your mobile home on your child's property, or

- communal living with your child and his or her family.

It is a good idea to write out all the pros and cons of making such a move as it affects your and your loved ones' lifestyles dramatically. Make sure all of you are clear about all of your expectations and work out any concerns in advance. This will minimize misunderstandings and, if you choose to go ahead with this option, help smooth the transition.

Housing Options for Semi-Active Retirees

Still healthy and mobile, your next phase of retirement may involve you switching to a lifestyle that is more passive. You will now be fully retired from business or part-time work, and will be traveling less. You are staying closer to home and near your loved ones. You've traded in your RV or houseboat and have moved into a nice condo or mobile-home park. You are at a stage where you may require nonprofessional assistance such as housekeeping, yard help, and meal-preparation services.

Option 3: Assisted home care

Most retirees prefer to prolong their stay at home for as long as possible, and the assisted home-care option allows them to do just that. This option is a logical choice for you if you require only minimal non-professional assistance, such as housekeeping services and help with running errands.

It is an ideal option if you do not wish to burden your loved ones with the routine simple tasks of your daily living. Consider an arrangement whereby a home-care worker comes in on a regular basis and attends to chores you do not wish or are unable to attend to yourself.

This option is usually much more affordable than moving into a retirement home, especially if your spouse is still healthy and living with you independently. Nonetheless, it's prudent to check with your local government authorities to see if any or all of the costs may be subsidized or covered.

Option 4: Independent-living retirement homes

This option is most suitable for retirees who are just beginning to move from semi-active to passive retirement. An independent-living retirement home is usually professionally managed, well-maintained, and peaceful. It provides you with an individual apartment in a residential complex, with provisions for two to three prepared meals a day in a cafeteria or restaurant-style setting. Most homes encourage residents to interact with each other and to maintain a healthy lifestyle, and offer a variety of daily activities and programs for their residents.

Most feature programs such as yoga and stretching, pottery and arts classes, and have frequent outings for picnics, movies, and plays. Transportation is usually arranged by the retirement home and is usually included in the monthly charge. Some high-end communities even have their own golf courses, on-site beauty salons and spas, and daily live entertainment. Some are virtually all-inclusive resorts or can be described as cruise ships on land.

It is important that you select your retirement community very carefully. Find one that can provide you with the comfort level you desire and that is within your budget. You really must shop around. Compare locations, quality, and the type and variety of services offered. Pick the one that best matches your ideal lifestyle for your particular phase of retirement.

Here are some questions to think about before making your move:

- What type of retirement home is most suited to your needs and interests?
- Do you like to have people around all the time?
- Do you think you can fit in with the existing residents?
- Can you handle the noise level of apartment living?
- How far away is the retirement home from your closest loved ones? (If you wish to maintain a close relationship

with your family, ideally you should live no more than 30 minutes from them.)

- What services and facilities does the retirement home offer? Are they of interest to you?
- Will you be paying for services you will not use?
- Do the residents appear happy and content? (Check out a few retirement homes and compare.)
- Does the staff seem trustworthy? Friendly? Professional?
- What is the cost, and can you afford it?

Use Checklist 1: Independent Living Retirement Home: Evaluation and Inspection to help you with your review and comparison. (Checklist 1 is included online at <www.self-counsel.com/updates/after55/bonus/htm>.) Don't forget to ask questions, and keep asking them until you have enough information.

Housing Options for Passive Retirees

Option 5: Assisted-living retirement homes

Assisted living is the next level of care available to you, should you require it. An assisted-living retirement home usually has full-time health-care professionals to help you with your medical and personal care, such as bathing or showering, dispensing medications, or other minor nursing functions. Often, such facilities are connected to independent-living retirement homes, so that as residents move from semi-active to passive retirement, their transition is more seamless and less stressful.

The extra cost for an assisted-living retirement home is still considerably cheaper than moving into a full-service extended-care home.

If possible, it is best that you personally visit several homes before making your choice. You will probably want to go with your spouse or partner, or with a relative or close friend who can help you make an objective selection.

Make an appointment for your first visit. You will probably be escorted and shown the facilities. Usually there will be someone there to answer your questions. Take your time; a hasty visit won't help you make the best decision.

Do revisit the home unannounced at another time. This will give you a second look at the retirement home as it normally is. Do the residents still appear healthy and happy? Or do they appear more stressed and depressed than your initial tour visit? Does the staff still seem friendly and helpful? These are telltale signs as to whether the retirement home is well run or not.

Checklist 2: Assisted-Living Retirement Home or Long-Term Care Facility: Evaluation and Inspection for review and comparison purposes. (Checklist 2 is included online at <www.self-counsel.com/updates/after55/bonus/htm>.) Again, don't forget to ask lots of questions until you have all the answers to make an objective decision.

Option 6: Extended-care or long-term care homes

At the most advanced stage of your passive retirement, you may be fully dependent on other people for daily living and care. You will probably require mobility assistance. You may have severe chronic disabilities and/or illnesses that require round-the-clock professional care. Extended-care homes provide this level of care. This is one of the costliest retirement housing options.

Ideally, it is best that you personally visit several homes before making your choice. More often than not, however, at this stage in your life, you will have to depend on your spouse or partner, grown children, close relatives, or friends to help you make an objective selection.

Whoever you designate to check facilities for you, have him or her use Checklist 2: Assisted-Living Retirement Home or Long-Term Care Facility: Evaluation and Inspection for review and comparison purposes. Again, don't forget that you or your representative should ask lots of questions. Make sure you (or your loved ones) have all the answers you need before making that all-important decision about where you will be living for the rest of your life.

You really must begin your housing research as early as possible in your retirement. There may be government subsidies and support available in your community, state, or province for certain housing options. The earlier you check into their availability, the better off you'll be.

The places you choose for each different stage in your retirement life will be your homes. It is worth the effort to seek out the ones that will best suit your needs.

Keep in mind that no home is perfect and none will be likely to fulfill all your needs and expectations. Nonetheless, it is possible to find one that's closest to your desired lifestyle and within your budget. You just need to do your homework and invest a bit of time in your search.

For more information on passive-retirement housing options, check out *Making the Right Move: Housing Options for Seniors*, also published by Self-Counsel Press.

Chapter 10
ESTATE PLANNING

A truly thorough retirement plan will include estate planning. Estate planning involves the creation and completion of legal and financial documents concerning end-of-life issues. By creating an estate plan, you will save your family and loved ones a great deal of anxiety at a time when they can least cope with it.

Proper planning on your part can help to secure your family's future financial security. In addition, it can minimize or eliminate estate and other final return taxes.

The following items should be on your things-to-do list:

1. *Write out a will and keep it updated.* If you don't have a will, you give up control over how your estate will be distributed. You give up the right to choose your estate's beneficiaries, to appoint your preferred executor and trustee, to designate a guardian for your minor children, and to make specific gifts to friends and relatives. Another consideration is that changes in the tax law may affect your estate, which may result in your estate having to pay more taxes and probate fees — and your family being left with a smaller share

of your assets than you wished them to have. To ensure your will stays current, you should review it annually.

2. *Draw up a power of attorney.* A power of attorney is a document that gives someone authority to act as your agent on your financial matters, should you become incapable of acting for yourself. It is usually set up at the same time as you draft your will. If you are in a stable relationship, you can assign your power of attorney to your partner. If you are not, a trusted relative or friend may be chosen instead.

3. *Draw up a living will.* Also called an advance directive or a health-care directive, this is a document that states how you wish to be treated, should you become incapacitated by illness, injury, or old age. Your living will covers procedures that may prolong your life but not cure you. Typically, the document requests that —

   • all life-prolonging measures be rendered, or

   • all life-prolonging measures be withheld, or

   • some mixture thereof be rendered, and

   • you be provided with "comfort care," including pain medication.

   These directives allow you to make decisions well ahead of your final illness. They also relieve your family of the burden of making painful life and death decisions for you.

4. *Name your beneficiaries on assets you may own.* These assets may include bank accounts, qualified or registered retirement accounts, and life insurance policies.

5. *Take the time to select the right executor for your estate.* First ask for that person's permission before naming him or her as the executor of your estate. Your executor should be trustworthy, financially prudent, and not be likely to predecease you. Keep in mind that the

person who accepts the role of executor will be personally and totally liable for your estate's affairs. It may be wise to consider naming a trust company to be your estate's coexecutor.

6. *Build up sufficient financial resources for your estate's final expenses.* These final expenses include inheritance and other taxes, funeral arrangements, probate fees, money to pay off any and all debts, and other costs of administering the estate after death. Throughout this book, ways to build up financial resources have been discussed.

7. *Prepare an up-to-date inventory of your assets, debts, and important papers.* You should update this inventory at least once a year. Some of the more important items in this inventory will include —

   - bank accounts (include account numbers and locations),
   - ownership papers (include the deed to your house and other properties),
   - credit card numbers,
   - life insurance policy papers, and
   - location of your safety deposit box.
   - Use Checklist 3: Personal Contacts and Inventory to inventory all your important papers and information. (You'll find this checklist online at <www.self-counsel.com/updates/after55/bonus.htm>.)

8. *Take time to communicate your wishes to your family.* Include them in the decision-making process. Doing so will minimize the possibility of a family member challenging your will after your death. Take care that everyone understands the will and the reasons for your bequests.

9. *Take time to learn about estate planning.* Read books and attend workshops. Consult with professionals when needed. Keep informed of tax changes and talk to estate- and financial-planning experts.

10. *Don't ignore life!* Do take time to smell the roses. Enjoy your loved ones today.

Knowing as much as you can about estate planning is essential to your loved ones' future financial well-being. For more information on wills, powers of attorney, and estate planning, see *Write Your Legal Will in 3 Easy Steps* (US and Canada) and *Power of Attorney Kit* (Canada only), also published by Self-Counsel Press.

Appendix 1
FREE MONEY AND OTHER SAVING TIPS

Hurry, hurry, read all about it! This chapter offers you all kinds of money-saving ideas and tips to help you keep more of your dollars in your pocket. (Please note that actual savings or benefits may change or be discontinued without notice.)

For Both Younger and Older Retirees

If you're 65 or older, check out the following list for freebies, discounts, and other money-saving opportunities. You may qualify for some of these savings even if you're as young as 50!

Discounts

AARP discounts

Toll free: 1-888-687-2277
Website: www.aarp.org/benefits

Big savings are available for AARP members, offered by many merchants. Some examples include the following:

   (a) US Airways (20 percent to 50 percent)

(b) Avis, National, and Hertz car rental discount (5 percent to 30 percent)

(c) Major hotel chains savings (10 percent to 50 percent)

(d) Reebok — Rockport outlet store discounts (20 percent)

(e) Gateway computers (7 percent off) and training (35 percent off)

(f) Various legal and financial services

CARP discounts

Website: www.50plus.com

Check out the savings available to Canadian CARP members from CARP's website.

Seniors' discounts

Website: www.seniordiscounts.com

More than 125,000 discounts are available across the US. This website searches for discounts in your area using your zip code and search category. Check out the following:

(a) Southwest Airlines offers seniors over 65 fare discounts of 20 percent to 65 percent. Fares are completely refundable, and do not require advance purchase.

(b) Value Village in Seattle offers seniors older than 62 a 20 percent discount off all used merchandise.

(c) Kohl's Department Stores give seniors older than 62 a 10 percent to 15 percent saving on purchases made on selected Wednesdays.

(d) IHOP restaurants offers a 10 percent discount to seniors older than 55. A seniors' menu with smaller portions is also available.

Free

Free eye care: Eyecare America

Toll free: 1-800-222-3937
Website: www.eyecareamerica.org/eyecare

Go to their public service programs link to find out how to access free medical eye care and eye-health educational materials for seniors. (Free care for those older than 65 years of age, who have not seen an ophthalmologist in the past three years, and who do not belong to HMO or the VA.)

Local community service organizations such as the Lions Club and the Kiwanis often offer free eye-exam clinics for low-income seniors. Check with their local offices.

Free dental care

Check with your local universities and colleges for their dental schools. Often, free or subsidized dental care by apprenticing students is available for seniors.

Free health care

Toll free: 1-800-411-1222
Website: www.cc.nih.gov/

National Institutes of Health Clinical Center is the center for testing the newest medical procedures. There are usually a number of programs under study and testing for diseases such as cancer, Alzheimer's, and heart conditions. You may qualify for free health care at their hospital in Bethesda, Maryland.

Free prescription drugs from pharmaceutical companies

Pharmaceutical Research & Manufacturers of America

Website: www.phrma.org

Free medication to low-income individuals with no drug coverage, regardless of age.

Cost Containment Research Institute

Website: www.institutedc.org

Free and Low-Cost Prescription Drugs booklet

This publication lists hundreds of free and discount medications.

Mail $6.00 to:

Institute Fulfillment Center
Prescription Drug Booklet #PDB-370
Box 210
Dallas, PA 18612–0210

Prescription drug discounts

Medicare drug discount cards (up to $30 per year)

These cards can often save you 10 percent to 25 percent off prescription drugs, depending on the drug. There are many different cards for many different drugs, so check which card is appropriate for you before enrolling. You can get only one Medicare-endorsed drug discount card. They are available until 2006, when Medicare's Part D prescription drug benefit will take effect and these cards will no longer be necessary.

Together Rx (free)

Website: www.together-rx.com

This program offers discounts to Medicare participants who don't have prescription drug coverage.

Mail-order pharmacies

Often, you'll save money by buying from mail-order pharmacies.

Prescription-drug assistance programs

Website: www.benefitscheckup.org

For people age 55 and older, the National Council on the Aging provides a website listing available prescription-drug assistance programs.

Veterans Affairs

Veterans Affairs Health Benefits and Services (US)

Toll free: 1-877-222-VETS(8387)
Website: www.va.gov

Take advantage of available health and education benefits because of your past military services. Contact your local Veterans Administration Office of the US Department of Veterans Affairs.

Veterans Affairs Canada

Toll free: 1-866-522-2122
Website: www.vac-acc.gc.ca

There are various treatments and other health-related benefits available to veterans and their surviving partners. They include medical, surgical, and dental care; home adaptations; and other community health-care services.

Choice of hospitals

Website: www.jcaho.org/quality+check

When you have a planned hospital admission and have a choice of facilities, it is in your best interest to make some advance enquiries about the hospital. To ensure you will be receiving quality care at the lowest possible cost, select a non-profit, teaching hospital that is accredited by the Joint Commission on Accreditation of Healthcare Organizations (JCAHO). The accreditation assures you the facility meets certain required standards in its operations and in its delivery of care and services. A nonprofit, teaching facility will give you the highest level of care at the lowest possible cost.

Other Health Care Saving Tips

(a) *Take an aspirin a day:* Many studies have now confirmed that taking an aspirin a day is a healthy thing to do for your heart. Check with your physician before starting.

(b) *Floss and brush your teeth daily:* This daily regimen helps prevent cavities and gum disease, and minimizes your dental bills.

(c) *Consider using home remedies when safe to do so:* For curing or controlling certain minor discomforts, consider tried and true home remedies (such as, depending on the ailment, baking soda, fresh ginger, and other herbs). Consult the many home remedy resource guides available at your local libraries and on the Internet. **Note:** If you are taking medications, talk to your doctor before using any herbal or home remedies as they may conflict with your regular medication.

(d) *Buy generic drugs when that option is available:* Real savings can be achieved when you buy generic versus buying name-brand medications. Always ask whether a generic version of your drug is available before making your purchase.

For All Retirees

Here are some realistic, logical, and systematic saving ideas that can be painlessly incorporated into your everyday life.

General

- Avoid spending money on frivolous things or giving in to impulse purchases. Before making that "need to have" purchase, sleep on it overnight. Buy it only if you still want it desperately the next day.

- Buy only if you have the cash to pay for an item, even if you are using your credit card to make the purchase.

- Reduce or eliminate your magazine subscriptions. Go to your local public library to catch up on the latest edition of your favorite magazine. It's free!

- Save money by borrowing books and movies from your local public library.

- If you like to shop, go window shopping for fun but leave your money and credit cards at home.
- Shop in the off season, especially for clothing and seasonal items. Better-label clothing usually goes on sale between Thanksgiving and January.
- Quit smoking. This will not only help you save money on your life insurance premiums today, but also on potential future health care and medical costs.
- Keep your car for longer. Keep up with regular maintenance and refrain from trading in your current car for a newer model too soon. This can potentially save you thousands of dollars.
- Unplug or recycle that extra refrigerator in the storeroom or garage. Running this extra appliance can increase your electricity bill by up to 25 percent.
- To save energy costs, run your clothes washer and dishwasher only on full loads. Better yet, hang your wet laundry out to dry on a sunny day to save even more.
- Rent a video instead of going to the movies.
- Stay away from garage sales and auctions. You probably don't need any of the available items.
- Many restaurants offer free birthday dinners. Check with your favorite eatery to see if they offer this courtesy. Bring your ID for proof of your birth date.
- Make a commemorative video on the cheap. Videotape that special event by posting a request at film schools' bulletin boards. Senior students are willing to do it for a fraction of the professional price.
- Be a mystery shopper! You can be hired to shop and to eat out. It's a great way to get free products and services, and you may even get paid for your time!

Groceries and sundries

- Go grocery shopping on a full stomach. You'll find you buy less.

- Shop with a list. Don't stray, except to buy seasonal products you can use.

- Buy generic brands whenever possible. Their quality is usually equal to name brands, and you will save money.

- Reduce prepared food purchases. Make your meals from scratch. They are healthier and easier on your pocketbook.

- If you live in a large city, shop in ethnic grocery stores. Their prices are usually better.

- Make food in bulk quantities. Portion and freeze them in individual containers for later use.

- Grow your own vegetables, fruits, herbs, and flowers to save money.

- Shop for in-season food products. For example, buy and eat more fresh berries in the summer and root vegetables in the winter.

- Make your own household cleaners. You can expect to save many times over the cost of commercial brands. For example, to make window and glass cleaners, mix $\frac{1}{4}$ cup each of white vinegar and ammonia with $\frac{1}{2}$ bucket of warm water. Add a few drops of blue food coloring for a professional look. You can fill many spray bottles that cost only pennies each.

- Whenever possible, use coupons. They all add up to real savings. Download online coupons for additional savings.

- Audit your cash register tapes. Make sure you are charged the correct price at checkout. Pay special attention to advertised sale prices.

Banking and investing

- Each month, pay off in full your credit card bills to avoid paying outrageous credit card interest rates.

- Review the interest rates you're paying on all your debt, including credit card debt. Pay off the most expensive debt first. If you carry a balance, switch to a lower-rate credit card. Potentially, this can save you hundreds of dollars a year.

- Put your loose change into a glass jar at the end of each day. Deposit the proceeds into a savings account each month. You'll be amazed how fast it can accumulate. Invest 90 percent of this money every six months, or use it to pay down your debt. Reward yourself with the remaining 10 percent.

- Audit your bank charges. Compare different bank packages offered by the various banks. Bank charges differ tremendously. Some banks even offer free banking to retirees. Shop around.

- Always invest — seriously — any excess money that comes your way, including money received from the sale of assets and properties, unless it's needed for medical and other emergencies. It's too easy to mindlessly squander extra cash or windfalls.

- Be aware of interest-rate movements. Never pass up an opportunity to earn a higher rate of return. But be informed of the additional risk that you are required to take on. Ask if your bank offers any senior's rate premiums on savings and investments.

Travel and vacations

- Many cruise lines will give you a free trip in exchange for you presenting a lecture on your unique specialty or hobby. Often, cruises have themes, and your specialty may be a perfect fit. For example, get a free cruise by presenting a lecture on board about your unique investment style that has earned you an average annual return of 25 percent for the last decade!

- Discounted airline tickets can be obtained by signing on as package couriers for courier companies.

- If you are a passenger on an overbooked flight, and if the airline offers free flights to anywhere they fly to any customer who'll take the next flight, volunteer!

- Travel during off-peak seasons.

- Travel closer to home to save on transportation costs.

- Be a tourist in your own city, and save on transportation and accommodation costs.

- Become a tour guide.

- Organize a tour group. You can usually earn a free trip by arranging a group of people who want the same travel itinerary. The magic number is usually a minimum of 12 people.

- Work part-time for a cruise line. You can earn money and discounts on future cruises.

- Single men with dancing skills and good knowledge of etiquette are in demand on cruises. You can earn a free passage in exchange for providing single female passengers with your charm and platonic companionship.

- Join a discount travel club. You will be able to save as much as 50 percent on your travel costs including accommodations, meals, transportation, entertainment, and tourist attractions.

- Partner with another solo traveler to save on travel costs. A number of organizations will pair you with a traveling companion of similar personality and travel style.

- Shop the web for travel bargains.

- Frequent flyer programs are still a good deal and are getting better. Credit card companies will give you frequent flyer miles for using particular credit cards. Check and compare frequent flyer programs, and sign on for free and discounted travel.

- Many states offer seniors fishing and hunting licenses for free or at a 50 percent discount. Check with your local licensing bureau.

Appendix 2
LIVING WELL

A happy and satisfying retirement means learning to live well — and within your means. Here are some suggestions for getting the most out of your retirement.

Keep yourself occupied

The happiest retirees are the ones that lead full lives. They volunteer, have hobbies, and have a close connection with their communities, friends, and families. They love life. Find your passion and pursue it. See each day as an opportunity to live your life to its fullest.

Make a "to do" list

Nothing gets you out of bed and going faster than knowing you have things to accomplish. List your things to do each day; then, as a symbol of your achievements, check them off. Make your list of things to do achievable and practical.

Eat well

Watch your diet and follow the recommended portion size for your age, height, and weight. Eat a balanced diet unless otherwise advised by your doctor, and try to eat four or five small meals during the day instead of three large ones. It's more beneficial to your health, and better balances your blood sugar throughout the day.

Look for and eat in-season, locally grown fresh fruits and vegetables. Frozen versions are also rich in vitamins because, on harvest, they are quickly processed.

Health professionals recommend that you reduce your red meat intake and increase your consumption of fish and white meat. Especially curb your daily fat intake. Generally, no more than 30 percent of your daily calorie intake should be in the form of fat. Of that number, no more than 10 percent should come from saturated fat. Instead, use unsaturated fat, such as olive and grape seed oils.

Do not overeat. Moderate your meal portions and make sure each meal is well balanced. Many specialty cookbooks are designed to help create delicious, nutritious, and creative meals for one and two persons. You will also find easy recipes in libraries and on the Internet.

Stock up on healthy and easy-to-eat snacks, such as seasonal berries and other small fruits, cheese cubes, crackers, baby carrots, dried fruits, and health food mixes.

Drink alcoholic beverages in moderation, or as advised by your doctor, and drink plenty of water. Eight glasses a day is the recommended quantity, unless otherwise advised by your doctor.

Butt out

Smoking is bad for your health. Butting out is the best thing you can do. Your body will thank you for it from the day you quit. Studies have shown that when you quit smoking, you reduce your risk of lung cancer and pulmonary and heart diseases. Just think of the financial rewards you'll reap by not buying any more cigarettes. Treat yourself with some of those savings!

Exercise

There are many age-appropriate forms of exercise that are fun and can help you stay fit. Fitness experts highly recommend moderate daily exercise to combat cardiovascular disease, osteoporosis, and depression. Consult with your doctor before embarking on any exercise routine.

Swimming, Tai Chi, moderate weight training, and dancing are all excellent exercises for older adults. Yoga, too, is suitable and also improves the immune system.

Water aerobic classes, offered by community swimming pools, are popular with retirees. This form of exercise emphasizes low-impact cardio routines and gentle stretching.

A daily walk not only keeps you in better health, but it also gets you out of the house, helps you meet friends, and keeps you psychologically connected to your community. Early morning mall walking is a fun and popular way to exercise. The aisles are wide and safe, the air is temperature controlled year round, and you'll meet like-minded people for company and conversations. An hour of brisk walking three to four times a week helps you maintain your good health.

Rotate your exercise routine to keep dullness at bay. Periodically review your program to make sure it's still appropriate for you.

Connect with people

People are social creatures and benefit from human interaction. Make it a point to connect with others. Stay in touch with friends, neighbors, and your family. They are your connection to living well.

Make it a point to have friends who are not your ex-coworkers or individuals related to your work. Having friends from outside your working life can help make your retirement transition easier. Think about engaging in activities that help keep you physically fit, emotionally balanced, and spiritually satisfied. There are potential friendships lurking in every corner!

The Internet is another way to connect with others and the world. It is the high-tech method of staying in touch with family and friends. You can also check your community's events calendar. Attend shows, plays, and other group activities with neighbors and friends.

Consider volunteering in your community. Some volunteer possibilities include your local tourism office, libraries, museums, schools, airports, cruise terminals, and community centers.

There are many organizations that are always looking for enthusiastic and active retirees as volunteers. Check the Resources section of this book for the Corporation for National and Community Service. They operate three flexible programs under their Senior Corps:

- Foster Grandparent Program to help abused kids
- Senior Companion Program to help other seniors with daily tasks
- Retired and Senior Volunteer Program to generally help others

Breathe deeply

Practice proper breathing for better overall health. Many people forget to breathe, especially when they exercise.

Get annual physical exams

Be proactive with your health and schedule annual physical exams with your doctor. Many life-threatening and serious illnesses can be prevented or controlled if they are caught and treated in their early stages. Don't wait until you become really sick; often, that's what ruins your quality of life — not to mention your pocketbook.

Let your doctor know you wish to be reminded to come in for an annual checkup. Have his or her office call you for an appointment at about the same time each year.

Own a pet

Studies have shown a correlation between owning a pet and a person's happiness in life. Owning a dog or a cat provides you with companionship, lots of love, and a positive sense of responsibility. A dog also keeps you mobile, as you have to walk it at least twice a day.

Stay informed

Turn on the TV, the radio, and/or the Internet. Find out what's happening in your community and around the world. It'll make you a more interesting person. Staying informed also gives you a sense of belonging.

Pursue personal growth

Continue developing your skills. Just because you're retired doesn't mean you should stop learning. Indulge in your favorite hobby. Take classes and workshops to help you become good at it. Learn things that give you satisfaction.

Have a safety network

If you are single, arrange to have someone check in on you on a regular basis. This person could be one of your grown children, or another family member, or a friend or neighbor. Arrange with a buddy to call each other up to make certain each of you is OK. Knowing you're secure will not only give you peace of mind, but will also give you a sense of belonging to the larger community.

Be financially sound

Financial independence will give you a good feeling. Be financially savvy and live within your means. Debt-ridden retirees undermine their own quality of life and cultivate worries and stress-related illnesses.

Simplify your life

Consider having a yard sale to get rid of clutter. Those things you've been holding onto but not using will be better off in someone else's possession. Recycle and pocket the cash.

Alternatively, you can donate things you don't use to charities and goodwill associations. It'll make you feel good.

Here's a good rule to keep in mind to help you minimize clutter: One item must go before another item can come into the home.

Appendix 3
HOME SWEET; HOME SAFE

Most retirees want to stay in their current homes. In fact, 83 percent of older North Americans wish to spend the rest of their lives in the homes they have now. Unfortunately, most homes are not designed to accommodate the needs of people aged 65 and older.

Therefore, upgrading your home to accommodate your changing needs is crucial to your safety, comfort, and security. Conduct a safety audit on a regular basis, preferably once a year, with the help of an occupational therapist.

The greatest threats to independent living for aging retirees are falls and the injuries that result from them. Often, you are not aware of the potential dangers around your home. For example, you could prevent a fall by replacing a slippery bathmat with one that has a rubber, nonslip bottom.

According to the Rehabilitation Engineering and Assistive Technology Society of North America (RESNA), <www.resna.org>, home modifications should improve the following features of a home:

1. Accessibility
2. Adaptability
3. Visibility
4. Universal design

Take an objective look at the home in which you are now living, or at any home you're considering moving to, bearing in mind each of the safety issues mentioned below.

Bathrooms

- Are there secured handrails to aid you in getting in and out of the bathtub and shower?
- Is the flooring nonslip?
- Do all faucets have anti-scald valves to prevent scalding?
- Is the shower thermostatic to control water temperature?
- Is the bathtub/shower a walk-in?
- Are the faucets easy to use?

Kitchen

- Is there a sturdy, nonslip step stool for reaching objects in higher cupboards?
- Is the fire extinguisher within easy reach? Do you know how to use it?
- Does the kitchen have a working smoke alarm?
- Is the flooring nonslip? (Do not use scatter rugs.)
- Is there adequate lighting above all work surfaces and eating areas?

Bedroom

- Is there a telephone in the bedroom? Keep important phone numbers by the telephone by the bed; pre-program speed-dial numbers to close relatives and neighbors. Memorize them and 9-1-1.

- Does the telephone have a large-numbered keypad?
- Does the room have gas and smoke alarms?
- Is there a flashlight beside the bed?

(**Tip:** If applicable, look into personal SOS devices that can be worn around the neck. Do wear one to bed. Do not hesitate to use it. Medic Alert and Lifeline are companies that sell these devices.)

Around the Home

- Is your home on one level?
- Does it have adequate lighting both around the perimeter and throughout the home? (Where appropriate, set up automatic timers for lighting to provide security and conserve energy.)
- Does it have motion sensor lights around the perimeter?
- Is the doorbell in good working order and set at a volume that can be heard in every part of the home?
- Are there peepholes or viewing panels on the doors? Are they right for your height?
- Does the house have an alarm system?
- Is the shrubbery trimmed back near doorways and windows?
- Do the doors have lever handles instead of knobs?
- Are the floors kept clear of clutter to prevent accidental tripping?
- Are the rugs either nonskid or tacked down? (Avoid scatter rugs, if possible.)
- Are all electrical cords kept rolled up and out of the way?
- Are all extension cords in good condition?
- Are all electrical outlets properly grounded to prevent shocks?

- Do all stairways — inside and outside — have secured handrails?
- Do you keep important phone numbers by all the telephones around your home? (Preprogram speed-dial numbers to close relatives and neighbors whenever possible.)
- Do you know your neighbors?

When away on Vacation

- Set up automatic timers on your lighting, radio, and television to give the impression of someone being at home.
- Put your regular mail on hold, or redirect its delivery to a temporary postal address.
- Cancel all home deliveries.
- Have a neighbor and/or relative periodically check in on your home. Ask them to clear away any stray flyers and mailers from the front door.
- Consider getting a house-sitter.

Other Securities/Cautions

- Often retirees are vulnerable to various direct solicitations. Watch out for telemarketers, direct-mail solicitations, television infomercials, televangelists, and other potential predators.
- Be wary of and watch out for door-to-door scam artists,
- Never give out personal information over the telephone, the Internet, or at the door unless you can independently verify the legitimacy of the organization that has approached you.
- Wear ID jewelry or a medic-alert if you have medical conditions that paramedics and others should know about, should an emergency occur.

RESOURCES

US Resources

AAA (American Automobile Association)

Website: www.csaa.com

A not-for-profit organization offering a wide array of automotive, travel, insurance, and financial services to its members and the public in North America.

AARP (American Association of Retired Persons)

Toll free: 1-888-OUR-AARP (1-888-687-2277)
Website: www.aarp.org

A nonprofit, nonpartisan member organization devoted to the health and well-being of adults of more than 50 years of age. AARP provides a wide range of services, benefits, and resources to its members. It is also a leader in advocacy for people older than 50.

Administration on Aging (AoA)

Telephone: (202) 619-0724
Website: www.aoa.gov

AOA is the Federal focal point and advocate agency for older persons and their concerns. Through information and referral and outreach efforts at the community level, AOA seeks to educate older people and their caregivers about the benefits and services available to help them.

Alzheimer's Disease Education & Referral Center (ADEAR Center)

Toll free: 1-800-438-4380
Website: www.alzheimers.org

Distributes free information and publications about Alzheimer's disease to health professionals and the general public.

American Medical Association

Toll free: 1-800-621-8335
Website: www.ama-assn.org

The website offers a wealth of information about individual doctors, their training, and specialties. State licensing boards can usually be located through the AMA. This may lead to important information about your doctor, including information on actions and malpractice claims, as well as disciplinary records, if any.

BenefitsCheckUp®

Website: www.benefitscheckup.org

A free and confidential service offered by the Council on the Aging to provide you with a personal report of available public programs and benefits you may qualify for. It has a comprehensive online helper to assist you to screen federal, state, and some local private and public benefits for older adults (aged 55 and older).

Centers for Medicare and Medicaid Services

Website: www.cms.hhs.gov

A free service providing you with free information and booklets about Medicare coverage and other health-related topics.

Corporation for National and Community Service

Telephone: (202) 606-5000
Website: www.seniorcorps.org

An organization that manages Senior Corps., a group that recruits and coordinates senior volunteers for their programs:

- Foster Grandparent Program
- Senior Companion Program
- Retired and Senior Volunteer Program

Cost of living comparison – Sperling's BestPlaces

Website: www.bestplaces.net

This website offers you a comparison of the cost of living among various cities across the country. It is based on various data sources including federal and state governments.

Eldercare Locator

Toll free: 1-800-677-1116
Website: www.eldercare.gov

A free public service of the US Administration on Aging. It provides information on different aspects of caregiving, aging, and other related issues.

Elderhostel

Toll free: 1-877-426-8056
Website: www.elderhostel.org

An organization that offers travel and travel-related educational programs for seniors around the world.

Elderweb

Website: www.elderweb.com

An award-winning online resource to help you use the rest of the Internet to access information related to eldercare and aging issues.

Internal Revenue Agency (IRS)

Website: www.irs.gov

The Internal Revenue Service is the nation's tax collection agency and administers the Internal Revenue Code enacted by Congress. IRS Taxpayer Assistance Centers are your one-stop resource for face-to-face tax help.

Joint Commission on Accreditation of Healthcare Organizations (JCAHO)

Website: www.jcaho.org

An independent, not-for-profit organization setting standards and evaluating the quality and safety of care for nearly 16,000 health care organizations in America. Consumers can access quality check results of various types of care providers, including hospitals, long-term care facilities and home care organizations.

Meals on Wheels Association of America

Telephone: 1-703-548-5558
Website: www.mowaa.org

A program that delivers free meals to your home. Anyone aged 60 and older is eligible.

Medicare

Toll free: 1-800-633-4227
Website: www.medicare.gov

A federal health insurance program for people aged 65 years or older. Its website provides information on eligibility, helpful contacts, prescription drugs, and other assistance programs.

National Academy of Elder Law Attorneys

Website: www.naela.org

A nonprofit association that assists lawyers, bar organizations, and others who work with older clients and their families. It provides a resource of information, education, networking, and assistance to those who deal with the many specialized issues involved with legal services to the elderly and people with special needs.

National Council on the Aging (NCOA)

Telephone: 202-479-1200
Website: www.ncoa.org

The National Council on the Aging is a national, nonprofit group of people and organizations dedicated to promoting the dignity, independence, well-being, and contributions of older people.

Retirement Living Information Center

Website: www.RetirementLiving.com

A website that offers you specific information on taxes and rates in the various states. It is operated by Retirement Living Information Center, an organization established to assist seniors in living out their retirement years.

Senior Community Service Employment Program (SCSEP)

Toll free: 1-877-872-5627
Website: www.doleta.gov/seniors/

Provided by the us Department of Labor's Employment & Training Administration, various federal programs offer part-time training and employment opportunities for eligible low-income persons 55 and older.

US Department of Veterans Affairs

Website: www.va.gov

A host of benefits and resources are available to eligible veterans of the United States armed forces. Check out their website or contact your nearest VA facility office.

US Department of Housing and Urban Development (HUD)

Website: www.hud.gov

A federal department with a mission to support community development and increase access to affordable housing. Check your local phone directory for its state office number.

US Social Security Administration

Toll free: 1-800-772-1213
Website: www.ssa.gov

The administration provides a wealth of information on your social security benefits and how the system works. It has on-line calculators to help you figure out your best retirement course of action.

Utah State University's Assistive Technology Program

Website: www.aginginplace.org

Information on the latest assistive technologies in growing older in the comfort of your home.

Wheelers RV Resort & Campground Guide

Website: www.wheelersguides.com

Listings for the United States, Canada, and Mexico, describing and locating government and privately operated parks serving campers and RVers. Private enterprise parks and campgrounds are rated with one to five stars, with five being the highest.

Canadian Resources

CAA (Canadian Automobile Association)

Website: www.caa.ca

A not-for-profit organization offering a wide array of automotive, travel, insurance, and financial services to its members and the public in North America.

CARP (Canada's Association for the Fifty-plus)

Website: www.50plus.com

CARP stands for Canadian Association of Retired Persons. However, the name no longer describes CARP's membership, who are aged 50 years or older, retired or not.

Canada's largest 50-plus lobby group, CARP speaks out on many issues important to those older than age 50. It provides a wide range of services, benefits, and resources to its members.

Canada Mortgage & Housing Corporation (CMHC)

Website: www.cmhc.ca

A government of Canada national housing agency. It also provides assistance to seniors through various assisted housing programs.

Canadian Association for Community Care (CACC)

Website: www.cacc-acssc.com

A national, nonprofit, and bilingual association committed to providing a strong national voice for the community-care sector.

Canadian Snowbird Association

Toll free: 1-800-265-3200
Website: www.snowbirds.org

The CSA is a national and international nonprofit organization created to represent the health care, social, and economic interests, and the needs and concerns of Canadians who travel.

Canada Revenue Agency (CRA)

Toll free: 1-800-959-8281
Website: www.cra.gc.ca

This government agency administers tax laws for the Government of Canada and for most provinces and territories, and various social and economic benefit and incentive programs delivered through the tax system.

Canadian Home Income Plan (CHIP)

Toll free: 1-800-563-2447
Website: www.chip.ca

Canadian Home Income Plan Corporation is Canada's first and only national provider of reverse mortgages for seniors.

How to Care

Website: www.howtocare.com

A website from one caregiver to other caregivers in Canada. It offers good resources and information on caregiving and aging.

Health Canada

Telephone: (613) 957-2991
Website: www.hc-sc.gc.ca

A free public service of the Federal Government of Canada. It provides information and resources on various aspects of public health and related care. It has six regional offices, providing bilingual services across the country.

Seniors Canada On-line

Website: www.seniors.gc.ca

Canada's trusted source of senior-related information on the Internet.

Social Development Canada (SDC)

Website: www.sdc.gc.ca

A government administration overseeing Canada Pension Plan benefits and Old Age Security benefits. Contact your regional offices for more information.

Veterans Affairs Canada

Toll free: 1-866-522-2122
Website: www.vac-acc.gc.ca

A host of benefits and resources is available to eligible veterans of the Canadian armed forces. Check out their website or contact your nearest regional office.

Other Reading from Self-Counsel Press

Making the Right Move: Housing Options for Seniors
by Gillian Eades Telford, RN, BSN, LTCAC, MES

Sell Your Home in Canada
By Geraldine Santiago

Simply Essential Personal Budgeting Kit
By Sylvia Lim, CFP®, CGA

Simply Essential Family Records Kit
By Liberty Craig

Write Your Legal Will in 3 Easy Steps
American version by Craig Waters, Attorney
Canadian version by Tom Carter, Attorney

You will find the following bonus Worksheets, Checklists, and Glossary by going to Self-Counsel Press's website at <www.self-counsel.com/updates/after55/bonus.htm>.

Checklists

1. Independent Living Retirement Home: Evaluation & Inspection
2. Assisted Living Retirement Home or Long-Term Care Facility: Evaluation & Inspection
3. Personal Contacts and Inventory

Worksheets

1. Retirement Goal Planning
2. Net Worth
3. Income-Producing Investments
4. Cash Inflow (for active and semi-active retirees)
5. Cash Inflow (for passive retirees)
6. Yearly Spending Budget (for active retirees)
7. Yearly Spending Budget (for semi-active retirees)
8. Yearly Spending Budget (for passive retirees)
9. Home Downsizing Comparison

Glossary